Clerks

This study of Kevin Smith's debut film breaks new ground by exploring how *Clerks* sits at the intersection of political and cultural trends relevant to alternative youth cultures in the early 1990s.

Clerks (1994) was born of and appeals to a specific youth subculture, with the multimedia View Askewniverse developing out of the film's initial release. Drawing on existing texts and movements such as Richard Linklater's *Slacker* (1991), Douglas Coupland's novel *Generation X: Tales for an Accelerated Culture*, and alternative rock subcultures that had developed during and since the 1980s, the film presents a comedic take on working as a young person in 1990s America in a manner that was praised for its authenticity. Filmed on a miniscule budget, the roughness of the film's aesthetic combined with a hard rock soundtrack comprised of mostly independent bands convinced many that it could speak for young Americans, much more than polished, corporate Hollywood productions. The book situates the film within this wider cultural movement and cultural zeitgeist and explores the role of working-class youth and employment in the years following Reaganomics and its consequences as well as providing insight into the film's presentation of consumption and of its representation of masculinity and sexuality.

Clear, concise, and comprehensive, the book is ideal for students, scholars, and those with an interest in youth cinema, American independent film, Cult Film, Subcultures, and Counterculture, as well as both Film and American Studies more broadly.

Peter Templeton is Honorary Fellow of the School of Social Sciences and Humanities, Loughborough University. His research focuses on American literature and culture. He is also the author of *The Politics of Southern Pastoral Literature, 1785–1885: Jeffersonian Afterlives*.

Cinema and Youth Cultures
Series Editors: Siân Lincoln and Yannis Tzioumakis

Cinema and Youth Cultures engages with well-known youth films from American cinema as well the cinemas of other countries. Using a variety of methodological and critical approaches the series volumes provide informed accounts of how young people have been represented in film, while also exploring the ways in which young people engage with films made for and about them. In doing this, the Cinema and Youth Cultures series contributes to important and long-standing debates about youth cultures, how these are mobilized and articulated in influential film texts and the impact that these texts have had on popular culture at large.

Bande de Filles
Girlhood Identities in Contemporary France
Frances Smith

Gidget
Origins of a Teen Girl Transmedia Franchise
Pamela Robertson Wojcik

The Beatles and Film
From Youth Culture to Counterculture
Stephen Glynn

Clerks
'Over the Counter' Culture and Youth Cinema
Peter Templeton

For more information about this series, please visit: https://www.routledge.com/Cinema-and-Youth-Cultures/book-series/CYC

Clerks
'Over the Counter' Culture and Youth Cinema

Peter Templeton

LONDON AND NEW YORK

First published 2021
by Routledge
2 Park Square, Milton Park, Abingdon, Oxon OX14 4RN

and by Routledge
52 Vanderbilt Avenue, New York, NY 10017

Routledge is an imprint of the Taylor & Francis Group, an informa business

© 2021 Peter Templeton

The right of Peter Templeton to be identified as author of this work has been asserted by them in accordance with sections 77 and 78 of the Copyright, Designs and Patents Act 1988.

All rights reserved. No part of this book may be reprinted or reproduced or utilised in any form or by any electronic, mechanical, or other means, now known or hereafter invented, including photocopying and recording, or in any information storage or retrieval system, without permission in writing from the publishers.

Trademark notice: Product or corporate names may be trademarks or registered trademarks, and are used only for identification and explanation without intent to infringe.

British Library Cataloguing-in-Publication Data
A catalogue record for this book is available from the British Library

Library of Congress Cataloging-in-Publication Data
A catalog record has been requested for this book

ISBN: 978-0-367-33354-6 (hbk)
ISBN: 978-0-429-31935-8 (ebk)

Typeset in Times New Roman
by Deanta Global Publishing Services, Chennai, India

Contents

List of figures vi
Series Editors' Introduction vii
Acknowledgements ix

Introduction 1

1 'Insubordination rules': *Clerks* and the counterculture
  of the 1990s 7

2 'A job that makes a difference': Youth and employment 24

3 'Who closed the store to play hockey?': Work and leisure 40

4 'I still get free Gatorade, right?': *Clerks*, youth,
  and consumption 56

5 'Any balls down there?': *Clerks*, slacker masculinity
  and sexuality 73

Conclusion 92

Bibliography 99
Index 105

Figures

1.1	Dante Hicks and Randal Graves in clothing typical of their subculture	18
2.1	Dante puts up his makeshift sign	34
2.2	Dante assists a customer	36
2.3	Another customer searches for 'the perfect box of eggs'	38
3.1	Dante and Randal prepare for a game of hockey on the roof of the store	44
3.2	A customer tries to trick Randal	46
3.3	Dante and Randal fleeing Julie Dwyer's wake	53
4.1	A 'customer' turns a crowd against Dante	62
4.2	The milkmaid, played by Smith's mother, Grace	65
4.3	Randal falls to his knees in joy at the 'good video store'	71
5.1	Veronica, wielding a fire extinguisher, rescues Dante	80
5.2	Veronica cradles Dante behind the counter	81
5.3	Jay and Silent Bob – Jay throws punches to the air	89

Series Editors' Introduction

Despite the high visibility of youth films in the global media marketplace, especially since the 1980s when Conglomerate Hollywood realised that such films were not only strong box office performers but also the starting point for ancillary sales in other media markets as well as for franchise building, academic studies that focused specifically on such films were slow to materialise. Arguably the most important factor behind academia's reluctance to engage with youth films was a (then) widespread perception within the Film and Media Studies communities that such films held little cultural value and significance and therefore were not worthy of serious scholarly research and examination. Just like the young subjects they represented, whose interests and cultural practices have been routinely deemed transitional and transitory, the films that represented them were perceived as fleeting and easily digestible, destined to be forgotten quickly, as soon as the next youth film arrived in cinema screens a week later.

Under these circumstances, and despite a small number of pioneering studies in the 1980s and early 1990s, the field of 'youth film studies' did not really start blossoming and attracting significant scholarly attention until the 2000s and in combination with similar developments in cognate areas such as 'girl studies.' However, because of the paucity of material in the previous decades, the majority of these new studies in the 2000s focused primarily on charting the field and therefore steered clear of long, in-depth examinations of youth films or was exemplified by edited collections that chose particular films to highlight certain issues to the detriment of others. In other words, despite providing often wonderfully rich accounts of youth cultures as these have been captured by key films, these studies could not have possibly dedicated sufficient space to engage with more than just a few key aspects of youth films.

In more recent (post-2010) years, a number of academic studies started delimiting their focus and therefore providing more space for in-depth examinations of key types of youth films, such as slasher films and biker films, or examining youth films in particular historical periods. From that point on, it was only a matter of time before the appearance of the first publications that focused exclusively on key youth films from a number of perspectives (*Mamma Mia! The Movie*, *Twilight*, and *Dirty Dancing* are among the first films to receive this treatment). Conceived primarily as edited collections, these studies provided a multifaceted analysis of these films, focusing on such issues as the politics of representing youth, the stylistic and narrative choices that characterise these films and the extent to which they are representative of a youth cinema, the ways these films address their audiences, the ways youth audiences engage with these films, the films' industrial location, and other relevant issues.

It is within this increasingly maturing and expanding academic environment that the **Cinema and Youth Cultures** volumes arrive, aiming to consolidate existing knowledge, provide new perspectives, apply innovative methodological approaches, offer sustained and in-depth analyses of key films, and therefore become the 'go to' resource for students and scholars interested in theoretically informed, authoritative accounts of youth cultures in film. As editors, we have tried to be as inclusive as possible in our selection of key examples of youth films by commissioning volumes on films that span the history of cinema, including the silent film era; that portray contemporary youth cultures as well as ones associated with particular historical periods; that represent examples of mainstream and independent cinema; that originate in American cinema and the cinemas of other nations; that attracted significant critical attention and commercial success during their initial release; and that were 'rediscovered' after an unpromising initial critical reception. Together these volumes are going to advance youth film studies while also being able to offer extremely detailed examinations of films that are now considered significant contributions to cinema and our cultural life more broadly.

We hope readers will enjoy the series.

Siân Lincoln & Yannis Tzioumakis
Cinema & Youth Cultures Series Editors

Acknowledgements

It has been a pleasure to write this book. In part this has been because it has allowed me to revisit a film important in my own youth. Just as significant, though, has been the fact that I have been fortunate enough to work with people who make the process a thoroughly enjoyable experience. I would be remiss if I did not mention here the contributions of the series editors, Siân Lincoln and Yannis Tzioumakis. They have shown enthusiasm from the project right from the start, and their hard work has helped me to refine ideas and produce a far better volume than it would have been without their input. I would also like to extend my thanks to Jennifer Vennall at Routledge for her part in making this a smooth process.

This would also never have been possible without the education in film I received at Loughborough University and the opportunities that I had to teach film at that institution. I would like to thank Andrew Dix for both introducing me to film criticism back in 2004 and for his tireless support ever since; I would also like to thank colleagues such as Mary Brewer, Brian Jarvis, and Paul Jenner. I've had the pleasure to teach film with each of them, and in every case I am sure that I am a better scholar for the experience.

Introduction

In late 1994, Miramax Films released the movie *Clerks* and in the process launched the career of a first-time director, Kevin Smith. The film was initially made on a shoestring budget, with Smith famously maxing out a string of credit cards and selling his comic book collection to finance the film. Miramax, itself acquired little more than a year earlier by the Walt Disney Company, eventually threw its financial clout behind the film, raising the budget significantly – not least of all on an advertising blitz that gained the film far greater notoriety than would have been likely otherwise. On release, the film was a surprise hit at the Sundance Film Festival, with this success placing it at the heart of a wave of American independent cinema that included films such as *sex, lies, and videotape* (Soderbergh, 1989) and *Pulp Fiction* (Tarantino, 1994). Indeed,

> its success was also assisted by Miramax's decision to place the trailer in 800 prints of *Pulp Fiction*, targeting a particular youth demographic that was not expected to respond negatively to Smith's use of strong language or the quirky humour of the film's universe.
>
> (Tzioumakis 2006: 277)

Its success, combined with its relatively low production costs, meant that it made a profit many times over the initial outlay.

One of the things that led to this success was a claim to verisimilitude. *Clerks* is structured as a series of eighteen vignettes that dramatise the experience of working in a convenience store, with each section sign-posted by titles such as 'malaise,' 'lamentation,' and 'underground.' It was shot at night in the very convenience store in which Smith himself was employed, and *Clerks* received praise for the legitimacy with which it depicted the young people that were its focus. In his review of *Clerks* one month after its initial release, Roger Ebert wrote 'much has been written about Generation X and the films about it. *Clerks* is so utterly authentic that its heroes have never heard of their generation. When they think of 'X,' it's on the way to the video store' (Ebert 1994). One must take some care when following this line of thinking since notions of authenticity are known to be problematic when it comes to cinematic representation. Nevertheless, thinking about this film as 'true' to this generation has not disappeared; instead, it has entered some academic discourses, with one critic claiming more recently that the characters' 'banter is witty and authentic' (Tropiano 2006: 224).

In this book, I will not be arguing that *Clerks* is in some way 'authentic' in the manner of the quotations above but that discourses of authenticity are still a suggestive way into understanding the film's distinctive appeal as a product of a specific youth cultural grouping. At some level, this discourse might relate to *Clerks*' position as a central film in 1990s independent cinema. An oft-cited reason for the very existence of independent cinema is that it presents a version of the world and of America 'truer' than that which is provided by Hollywood, with Geoff King arguing that 'a strong tendency in one strain of American independent cinema has been towards the creation of a greater impression of reality or authenticity than is associated with the glossier style typical of Hollywood' (2005: 107). Initially, one might think that the perception of this film as authentic is a necessary component for it being successful within an independent cinema framework. This connection, though, does not by itself explain the film's popularity with younger audiences, given that critics and fans often frame independent cinema not merely as a departure from Hollywood productions but also as an alternative aimed primarily at an audience perceived as being more educated, discerning, and – crucially – older. As Michael Z Newman suggests, 'in contrast to Hollywood's youth audience or mass audience, the audience for independent cinema is generally mature, urban, college-educated, sophisticated' (Newman 2011: 38).

To understand *Clerks* as a youth film, then, one must consider it in the light of not only independent cinema but also the broader cultural phenomenon of 'Generation X.' When dealing with the American context, this group follows on chronologically from the 'Baby Boomers' and, while bracketing demographics is always an inexact science, is generally considered to include those born between the early 1960s and 1980. As a result, they would have been anywhere between 14 and 35 years old when *Clerks* was released in 1994. Critics such as Emmanuel Levy (1999: 208), Peter Hanson (2002: 79), and Samuel Amago (2007: 73) position *Clerks* as part of a cinematic trend relating to this demographic, in some cases along with the earlier film *Slacker* (Linklater, 1990). There is a significant connection between the two films; Smith himself credits seeing *Slacker* as the inspiration for his move into filmmaking.

I went to see a movie, Richard Linklater's 'Slacker' at the Angelika Film Center up in New York. And it was a real eye-opening experience, because it was not the standard studio fare that I was used to seeing everywhere, was weaned on. It was kind of my first independent film [...] I was fascinated by that. I viewed it with a mixture of awe and arrogance. I was awed by the fact that this passed for entertainment [...] that people would actually sit down and enjoy it as much as I was enjoying it. And then arrogance, because I was, like, 'Well, I could do this. I mean, if this counts as a movie, count me in, I can try this.'

('Interview with Kevin Smith' n.d.)

Slacker documented the lives of young people dealing with marginalisation and exclusion but who were too apathetic or disillusioned to do anything about it. The concept of this slacker mentality is the result of the historical timing of Generation X; they were born too late to participate in the radicalism of the 1960s and were left with the sense that for all the energy of the counterculture, the earlier generation had failed to achieve a better world. The result could manifest itself in either angry cynicism or a kind of apathetic withdrawal from the values of mainstream society but, in either case, this was perceived and characterised by older generations as a form of aimlessness:

> in the most pervasive stereotype, these 'slackers' are the Gen-X equivalent of hippies: they withdraw from the rat race as a half-assed rebellion against dehumanizing cultural forces. Yet slackers seek no revolutionary means for overturning or even healing the culture that appals them. Rebellious boomers hit the streets to demonstrate against misguided military actions, repressive politics, and other such ills, while slackers echo the previous generation's discontent but have neither clearly defined antagonizing forces nor clearly defined reactions to such forces.
>
> (Hanson 2002: 15)

As this book will demonstrate, the 'half-assed rebellion' is present in *Clerks* and is an actual accusation that one of the two primary 'slackers' levels at the other at the end of the film. The book will not ignore this but will work to interrogate the notion somewhat, not taking at face value the judgement of an older generation (even as that judgement is repeated by the text itself). Instead, it will consider the film and its representation of these young men and their lives in a broader socio-economic context than just the one depicted explicitly in the film.

In understanding *Clerks* as a product of Generation X, it is also important to look beyond the discipline of film studies. On the one hand, one must confront the material realities of the world experienced by this generation, which will enable a broader understanding of the world in which the film was created and the imprint that background noise had on the finished product. On the other hand, however, one must place emphasis on other manifestations of youth culture in this period, and on the further cultural presence of Generation X in the 1980s and early 1990s. One of the most crucial of these is the world of music. Indeed, other volumes in this series point to the telling interconnection between popular music and cinema in youth cultures.[1] *Clerks* is no different as the film undeniably bears the mark, both in its soundtrack and its – for the lack of a better word – *attitude*, of being created at a point where forces which had mainly been culturally underground had started to gain broader popularity. Grunge and other forms of 'alternative' rock had started displacing the glam metal and popular music that had dominated American record sales through the 1980s.

Grunge, likely the most significant instance of this alternative American rock music, has been said to reflect the social withdrawal seen elsewhere in the art of Generation X – to borrow Joshua Clover's description of the Nirvana song 'On a Plain,' 'this is the psychic landscape of quarantine, of over-determined inwardness, sequestered inside a disordered mind that is inside a body in turn removed from the public sphere' (Clover 2009: 85). Nevertheless, as much as this genre, and indeed the broader *zeitgeist*, might prioritise an examination of the internal psychodramas of American youth, it is probably far more telling that this genre inherits from punk rock an emphasis on both independence and authenticity. Consequently, *Clerks* emerges from a cross-genre movement with shared beliefs about art and its validity at a moment where those views are moving from the margins to the mainstream – as, indeed, is US independent cinema.

This book consists of five chapters and a conclusion. Chapter 1 seeks to place Smith's debut in a broader cultural context. Here, I will revisit some of the issues raised in this introduction to consider the film as part of a subculture that connected strains of American independent cinema with other cultural manifestations such as grunge music in a wider Generation X culture. The next two chapters deal with what is arguably the most crucial aspect of the film or which can at least be said to be its most overt concern: the world of work. Chapter 2 is driven by questions pertaining to materialism, dealing with realities of employment for the young and the kind of *ennui* that exists in what are, to borrow a phrase from Douglas Coupland's cult novel *Generation X* (1991) that others have used in this context, 'McJobs' (Hanson 2002: 72). Chapter 2, then, focuses on the film's explicit and implicit statements about employment in a post-Reagan economy, particularly for those young people who are, by virtue of their age and inexperience, initially trying to find their way in the world.

Chapter 3 pivots to observe that, though the film is shot in a workplace and with the primary two characters ostensibly at work, an awful lot of things that are not 'work' occur in their place of employment. Randal Graves (Jeff Anderson) spends more time in locations other than the video store he works in, and even when he is there, he spends more time entertaining himself than doing his job. His entire demeanour at work stands as a challenge to contemporary American consumer culture. Beyond this, we see the convenience store next door in which Dante Hicks (Brian O'Halloran) works is closed for an impromptu game of hockey on the roof, and so the two main characters can attend a wake. We see Dante unwind behind the desk with his girlfriend Veronica (Marilyn Ghigliotti), with change for customers left on the counter so that his relaxation will not be interrupted. Throughout the film, young characters engage far more with philosophical ideas and discussions of things that interest them than with their jobs. The film, then, rebels against the tenets of mainstream American culture and attitudes to 'hard' work in the 1990s by undercutting the seriousness of this work at every turn and by putting the more insightful points about their condition into the mouth of Randal, the more unrepentant of the two 'slackers.' The purpose of this chapter, then, is to consider the freeing potential of leisure at the workplace to counteract the misery of such 'McJobs.' In addition, it will explore what the film portrays as the self-importance of a culture that would have these two – and, by extension, the young people that they represent symbolically onscreen – treat exploitative jobs with more reverence.

Chapter 4 examines the representation of consumption in the film, an important topic since the two stores – a convenience store and a video store – are places dedicated to consumption, either of pop culture or of the myriad other items that Dante sells throughout the movie. Despite some pretty awful behaviour at times, the two main characters remain somewhat sympathetic because the expectations placed on them by their employers and members of the public far outstrip what either group could realistically expect of them. Much of the humour in the film stems from Randal's subversion of contemporary consumer culture, since, in a way, this subversion somewhat recalls Bakhtinian notions of carnivalesque; he has turned the situation on its head and runs the video store primarily for his own benefit and convenience. However, the two central characters are also avid consumers of pop culture. Though Randal especially could be viewed as something of an elitist in his attitude towards music and movies, we should not be blind to the fact that the consumption of pop culture that the two engage in daily is not a simple or passive experience; it has a depth that is not immediately apparent, in that it allows them to create and to make the workday tolerable.

Chapter 5, the final full chapter of the book, focuses on the world of sexuality and the masculinity of the film's protagonists. These are central concerns since, aside from the world of work, romance is one of the main driving forces in the narrative, while much of the comedy in the film relies on sex. The kind of masculinity – and indeed, the sexuality of these male characters – is somewhat complicated and unpacking its manifestations will be the concern of the chapter. Almost every discussion of sex involves something that blurs the boundaries of orthodox masculinity. Randal openly watches hermaphroditic pornography; the film's producer (Scott Mosier) plays a character nicknamed 'Snowball' due to his affinity for that particular sex act; Jay (Jason Mewes) talks about performing oral sex on Silent Bob (Kevin Smith) and other men before screaming in compensation about how much he loves women, and Dante admits to attempting to fellate himself. Although there is no explicit rejection of homophobia – by itself, the character of Jay and his routine use of homophobic insults and explicit misogyny would complicate any simple reading of slacker masculinity as 'progressive' – what is evident in the film is a willingness to go to areas not typically seen in mainstream cinema at the time. The film offers a more fluid representation of sexuality, one that can move seamlessly between partners of the opposite gender but that can more easily incorporate things which would otherwise be taboo. This break with orthodoxy is of great importance, both as a significant concern of youth cinema and the particular social dimension that arises from this presentation of masculinity being so different from the versions dominant in 1980s Hollywood.

Finally, the book will conclude by charting the film's wider cultural afterlife. This will include a brief look at *Clerks'* 2006 sequel, its existence in other media forms, and the wider cult following for the View Askewniverse, the diegetic world that connects most of Smith's films, including well-known titles such as *Chasing Amy* (1997) and *Dogma* (1999), which Smith also made in the 1990s. This following demonstrates that *Clerks* connected with youth audiences strongly enough to power a series of films which are now, necessarily, far removed from the independent status of the original. Taken as a whole, this volume will consider *Clerks* and other media sharing the same discursive universe as products of a specific youth subculture, with an appeal for that specific subculture that has grown along with the members of that distinctive social grouping.

Note

1 See for instance Brickman (2018) and Nelson (2019).

1 'Insubordination rules'
Clerks and the counterculture of the 1990s

As with any film, *Clerks* is no island, cut off from the rest of the world. To fully understand it, one must comprehend the conditions, both material and aesthetic, in play during the period of its creation. The need for this is doubly clear in the case of this particular film, as it arises from a matrix of various interpretations of 'independence' and what it means to be 'alternative' originating in various cultural and artistic forms. One might sensibly begin by considering this film as a manifestation of American independent *cinema*. Though an obvious move, this alone opens up a contentious debate about the nature of independent cinema in the US at that particular time and whether one should so clearly demarcate it from mainstream cinema. That critics do so culturally is clear, and 'at the heart of the process of definition is one of differentiation, as is the case with all cultural groupings' (King 2013: 47). However, much of the output labelled 'independent' may not necessarily deviate significantly from standard Hollywood fare; nor are Hollywood directors prohibited from borrowing from the toolbox of their independent counterparts. It becomes clear that, as in many independent films of the time, 'several aspects of the classical narrative and style remain in place. This means that in terms of aesthetics, independent films retain a certain grounding on mainstream traditions, the extent of which varies from film to film' (Tzioumakis 2006: 9). At first, one might initially see *Clerks* as a film that breaks with Hollywood norms quite substantially. It is shot in black and white and has only a faint rivulet of plot to anchor the film's various dialogue-heavy comic set pieces. However, Geoff King understands the film as a more conventional product:

> There is development in the narrative dimension, however, conforming to some more conventional dynamics. Dante seems at the end to be in the process of sorting out misunderstandings about his relationships with Veronica and Caitlin and is reconciled after a spat with

ultra-slacking neighbouring video-store clerk Randal (Jeff Anderson). Closure is effected literally, through the closure of the shop at the end of the day. This creates something of the kind of rhetorical closure frequently employed in Hollywood. It is heartfelt in some respects and not entirely ironic, although titles such as 'Catharsis' and 'Denouement' give it a self-conscious twist of a distinctly indie character.

(King 2005: 82)

Clerks, then, is not especially radical in terms of its form, or even its content, structured as it is around the heteronormative romances of its protagonist. Yet, despite this, the film is often considered a textbook example of independent cinema in this period. Part of this is undoubtedly the unusual manner of its production, which places it within an identifiable niche. Budget constraints had led to films being made more cheaply in the early 1990s than at earlier times in Hollywood's history. Around this time, a string of three microbudget features, each garnering notable success, led to

> a series of articles by Peter Broderick in *Filmmaker* magazine [and] served as a catalyst for the production of low-cost films, giving a detailed breakdown of each of the three budgets and underlining the strategies that permitted feature production at so little expense.

(King 2005: 12–13)

As a film made by a convenience store clerk who funded it by taking out a string of credit cards and selling his comic book collection, *Clerks* fits seamlessly with this discourse of low-budget American independent cinema that had emerged in the years preceding its production.

Another factor to consider is that Miramax handled the film's distribution. Founded in 1979 by Harvey and Bob Weinstein, Miramax had broken through as a significant player in the American cinematic landscape. Across the 1990s it was producing films that combined arthouse and popular sensibilities, and so it helped complicate the notion of an independent film as much as any other entity. Yannis Tzioumakis writes,

> Having made a name by releasing successfully a number of 'ideal' or paradigmatic independent films such as *sex, lies, and videotape* (Soderbergh, 1989), *Reservoir Dogs* (Tarantino, 1992), *Clerks* and *Dead Man* (Jarmusch, 1995), in recent years Miramax ha[d] shifted increasingly towards the finance and distribution of considerably more expensive, star-studded genre pictures.

(Tzioumakis 2006: 3)

This is a statement that not only indicates Miramax's growth away from this area but that positions *Clerks* within a lineage of 'independent output' by the company. In this case, the two might each be reinforcing the independent credentials of the other, with a film of this ilk serving to differentiate Miramax from their more family-friendly parent company (Disney). Meanwhile, the association with Miramax and its more radical catalogue, including work by Steven Soderbergh, Jim Jarmusch, and Quentin Tarantino, serves in turn to emphasise the quirkier, less conventional aspects of *Clerks* than its mainstream dimensions as identified by King above.

As crucial to this formulation, though, is the question of *attitude*. Such ethereal concepts are more difficult to approach and define than the material conditions of creation, which are minutely recorded and are easily traceable. However, while it is challenging to categorically classify the attitude of an artwork, in this case, it is an essential part of the 'independent' landscape, which is to say that this *milieu* is always figured as being in some way *against* something. If we follow the line set down by Pierre Bourdieu, we might see this as inescapable since

> tastes (i.e. manifested preferences) are the practical affirmation of an inevitable difference. It is no accident that, when they have to be justified, they are asserted purely negatively, by the refusal of other tastes. In matters of taste, more than anywhere else, all determination is negation.
> (Bourdieu 1994: 56)

In the case of independent cinema, however, the oppositional element is raised from an implicit attitude to a guiding *ideological* principle, one that advocates proudly wear on their sleeve:

> The value of indie cinema is generally located in difference, resistance, opposition – in the virtue of alternative representations, audiovisual and storytelling styles, and systems of cultural circulation. In many quarters, difference from Hollywood itself can be a mark of significant value. Indie film culture profits from its alterity, which sustains it and has the potential to be politically progressive and even counter-hegemonic. At the same time, this same culture functions to reproduce social class stratification by offering an elite, culturally legitimate alternative to the mass-market Hollywood offerings of the megaplex.
> (Newman 2011: 2)

This quotation from Newman is revealing because it offers us two ways into thinking about *Clerks* as an independent film. In the first sentence, one should note the idea of opposition that is central to the idea of 'indie.' Although Clerks does not necessarily reinvent the wheel in any formal respect, as it will be shown across the pages of this book, the film still adopts a stance towards the American mainstream that is largely oppositional, despite the presence of fundamental points of convergence between the two. The final sentence of this quotation indicates that though there is something potentially radical and progressive in this type of film, it simultaneously reinforces class division by offering a cultural experience that is elitist and produced for a *bourgeois* audience. Given the roots of the very particular independent cinema of the 1980s and 1990s in the arthouse, and the seemingly widely adopted notion that the very *popularity* of Hollywood is sometimes something to be held against it, the point being made here would seem to be true, at least in general terms. It is unclear, however, whether there is anything particularly elitist about *Clerks*, and indeed the tone of the film differs significantly from those produced by, say, Jim Jarmusch or Steven Soderbergh.

To account for this difference, one must think more broadly about what the primary target audience for *Clerks* was, moving beyond a conception of a straightforward binary opposition between high and low culture and considering a more diverse range of demographic factors. It is also helpful to remember that although one of the groups to whom independent cinema was marketed is this elite demographic that Newman identifies, 'the most significant audience for which Hollywood failed to cater in the immediate post-war decades, and which created the basis for some of the most important strains of independent production, was the youth audience' (King 2005: 6). It is, then, in this strain of youth culture that *Clerks* starts to make the most sense as a unique cultural product – and as one with the resonance to endure in the popular imagination well beyond the time of its creation.

Dealing with the particular generation for whom *Clerks* was especially significant brings us into contact with the demographic known as Generation X. These are people who could have been any age from their early teens to their early thirties at the time when *Clerks* was released, and indeed Kevin Smith himself, born in 1970, fits this description. Beyond their age, there are several recurring traits in the dominant popular discourse around Generation X. The first is that 'the rate of divorce per 10,000 women more than doubled from 1955 to 1975 and remained high throughout the Xer childhood years,' which meant the members of this group had a much greater chance of being children of divorce than any prior generation, something that supposedly changed their outlook on the world and on relationships (Richie 2002: 39–40). Second, there is a widely held idea that they were the first generation raised on television, and that 'Generation X has a much more extensive knowledge of television than any previous generation'

(Owen 1999: 6). Consequently, they were exposed to the rhythms and patterns of that medium – and of popular culture more broadly – from such a young age that little chance remains of their finding anything 'new' in any of these media formats. Both the outlook and media literacy of this group factor into efforts to understand what has often been referred to as 'Generation X cinema.' However, the most telling is the third point that cultural commentators refer to, which is the *attitude* of this group, who are seen by their elders as apathetic, cynical, and rebellious but in a disorganised and generally internalised fashion. For some, such as Peter Hanson, the roots of this are historical:

> Even the oldest Gen Xers were born too late to participate in the historical social unrest that reached its twilight in the mid-1970s, so all Gen Xers grew up in the aftermath of a beautiful but unrealised dream, and this sad fact informs their sensibility. Some wear this hand-me-down ennui as anger, some as cynicism, some as apathy.
>
> (Hanson 2002: 11)

For Hanson, what chiefly determines the condition of Generation X is their being born at that moment in American history. The 1960s had been a time of genuine political upheaval where young people had protested, and it had seemed as if alternatives to the prejudices of the past were possible. Members of Generation X had been too young to participate in that movement. They had seen instead the aftermath of the hippy movement and free love, which brought a pronounced counter-revolution in American society. Conservatism fought back with a vengeance from 1968, and the subsequent Presidential elections saw resounding victories for Richard Nixon (followed by the Watergate Scandal, which of course reinforced cynicism towards those in authority) and, with only a brief one-term interval for the Democrat James Carter, Ronald Reagan and George Bush. For Hanson, genuinely radical social change seemed an impossibility for Generation X because they had seen the last great movement founder, and their perceived powerlessness in the face of the American social juggernaut inspired little more than apathy.

Regardless of its origin, this preoccupation with the group's apathy is something that frequently recurs in commentary about this demographic. As Mwenda Ntarangwi suggests, 'the main characteristics of Generation Xers often pointed out in popular scholarship such as that of Douglas Coupland emphasize their apathy, slackness, and aimlessness' (2013: 86). There is, though, another way of seeing this representation of youth, one that critiques its emphasis on young people as being presumed as white, male, and middle class. Indeed, Traci Carroll reacts to a comparison between trends in grunge and hip-hop lyrics with the observation that part of the Generation X sensibility seems to derive from the fact that a widespread lack of economic opportunity, which has been a longstanding experience for African American youth, is now impacting large numbers of white youth for the first time.

(Carroll 2003: 204)

This suggests that the manifestation of elements associated with Generation X do not always account for questions of gender, race, and especially class, the last a concept not strongly privileged in a discussion of American youth, as is the case in other contexts such as the UK (see in particular Smith et al.). Indeed, outside the US the label 'Generation X' was not used widely to discuss particular youth demographics even though some of the key characteristics aligned with the ones identified with the American cohort (children of divorce, apathy, etc.).

Nevertheless, the conceptual framework of Generation X bears the burden of changes that took place in American society in the latter decades of the twentieth century. While previous generations had icons like Jack Kerouac or events such as the Woodstock Festival – countercultural icons and events that offered at least the *idea* of an alternative to mainstream culture – these alternatives no longer seemed plausible when viewed against the reach of corporate America. In fact, not only were these not plausible, but pre-existing iterations of American counterculture were no longer even desirable. A clear example of this appears early in the film *Reality Bites* (Stiller, 1994), broadly contemporary with *Clerks* and aimed at the same youth audience. As part of a valedictorian speech, the main character Lelaina Pierce (Winona Ryder) remarks, 'And they wonder [...] why we aren't interested in the counterculture that they invented [...] as if we did not see them disembowel their revolution for a pair of running shoes.' The Baby Boomers might well have seen Generation X as too lazy to inspire change, but this youth culture saw their predecessors as something much worse: sell-outs.

For many who chose to pathologise the collective apathy of this generation, the blame was laid on the fact that they were, overall, statistically far more likely to be children of divorce than their parents. It is in relation to this issue that the grouping is generally most treated as if they were a social problem; conservative commentators diagnosed their generational apathy as a symptom of the breakdown of the nuclear family. As an *Atlantic* article of 1992 put it, Americans born in 1961 'were the kindergartners who paid the price for America's new divorce epidemic' (Howe and Strauss 1992). In 1996, Gary Blair Zustiak would write that

> more than 40% of Generation X are children of divorce, compared to only 11% of those born during the 1950s [...] if they were given the

choice between an intact family with all of its problems and a divorced family with its lack of strife, the majority of kids would choose the intact family.

(Zustiak 1996: 43)

Journalistic positions of this kind from the early-to-mid 1990s arguably look somewhat dated today. Nevertheless, it is perhaps not stretching the case too far to suggest that a nihilist attitude – that the life of an American at this time could seem essentially *meaningless* – could be partly prompted by the collapse of an underpinning social narrative. The heteronormative romance – in which one meets someone of the opposite sex, falls in love, marries them, and grows old with them – had been one of the cornerstones of American culture and was one of the significant sacraments of life for many. Now, however, the whole ideological structure underpinning that sacrament began to collapse. If one worked to provide a better standard of life for the family, what did that mean when family *itself* was no longer fixed or absolute?

When diagnoses did not focus on their parents' marriages, they tended instead, as in Rob Owen (1999) and Karen Richie (2002), to find the underlying problem in the way that this generation consumed media. While the Baby Boomers reaped the rewards of the post-war economic surge in their youth, Generation X was raised in that climate from birth. This historical positioning has plenty of other consequences, but one of the most telling is its relationship with the media, with television well established as the dominant medium in the US by the 1960s. The argument that television went on to shape this generation rests on some rather determinist notions, and frankly, one might be wary about exactly how far such arguments can be accepted. Nevertheless, this level of engagement gave many in Generation X a tremendous amount of media literacy in terms of the programmes, films, characters, and plots that made up the popular entertainment of their youth. With this knowledge and the well-documented distrust of authority that Generation X often exemplified, one might see members of this group as examples of Henry Jenkins' textual poachers:

> Unimpressed by institutional authority and expertise, the fans assert their own right to form interpretations, to offer evaluations, and to construct cultural canons. Undaunted by traditional conceptions of literary and intellectual property, fans raid mass culture, claiming its materials for their own use, reworking them as the basis for their own cultural creations and social interactions.
>
> (Jenkins 1992: 18)

Beyond this, it is also well established that in the realm of art, there is a formal level, at least, at which one can see television's influence having an effect. The idea of a 'channel-hopping' aesthetic, one that moves erratically between narrative fragments rather than showing a story unfolding in a linear or 'classical' narrative style, is something which subsequently finds its way into other forms of postmodern art, such as cinema (as in the films of Tarantino and David Lynch, for example) and literature (in instances such as the writings of Robert Coover or Thomas Pynchon). But making the leap from recognising this formal innovation to providing an exact description of postmodernism is challenging, not least because here we are dealing with its iterations in several different media as part of an underlying cultural *milieu*. This difficulty is compounded by the fact that the term has been 'stretched in all directions across different debates, different disciplinary and discursive boundaries, as different factions seek to make it their own, using it to designate a plethora of incommensurable objects, tendencies, emergencies' (Hebdige 1988: 181).

One of the things with which scholars of postmodernism have had to contend is the usefulness of a term that can be so broadly applied, wondering indeed to what extent these various definitions share common traits. However, for the purposes of this volume, there are some significant harmonies between *narrative* versions of postmodernism that allow a scholar to approach a tentative definition. A key characteristic is that postmodern art becomes concerned with surfaces, what the notable critic of postmodernism, Fredric Jameson, referred to as 'a new kind of flatness or depthlessness, a new kind of superficiality in the most literal sense – perhaps the supreme formal feature of all the postmodernisms' (Jameson 1991: 9). For others, such as Jean Baudrillard, the blame for this lies – at least in part – with television. By beaming images directly into our homes around the clock, television leads to an overload of information. Baudrillard wrote in *Simulacra and Simulation* that 'We live in a world where there is more and more information, and less and less meaning' (Baudrillard 1994: 79). As with any other medium, television has its own conventions and tropes, and the constant bombardment of these images means that, for Baudrillard, they achieve a dominant position in society – or, to put this another way, they become 'more true than the truth, more *real* than the real' (Baudrillard 1994: 108). As the grand narratives that had organised society begin to come into question and fall away, the focus of art shifts towards popular culture itself. We can see this in *Clerks*, perhaps most famously in the lengthy discussions that the two protagonists have about *Star Wars* (Lucas, 1977) in particular.

Clerks, however, is not generally held to be a particularly postmodern film. Though the narrative is interrupted, and the form breaks with some of the conventions of classical Hollywood, there is little in the way of experimentation with time or character common to the films of David Lynch or Quentin Tarantino. The order in which events takes place is always clear, and the film does not make any real demand of the audience. It is also true that, while the protagonists discuss popular culture at length, as characters they are never reduced to stereotypes. This is not a film that prefers the flatness of TV clichés in the manner associated with high postmodernism. Though *Clerks* has some clear sympathies with postmodernism, there is still a need for another way of understanding this text, one more in tune with its distinctive tone and outlook.

This alternate approach is necessary because, in broader terms, if the reaction of both artists and audiences to the postmodern world had been homogeneous, then there would have been a profound contradiction at work within a postmodern Generation X culture. On the one hand, artists and film directors from Andy Warhol onwards had popularised what Best and Kellner call 'the postmodern turn,' in the process embracing the superficial nature of the contemporary world, challenging pre-existing views of art that prioritised an idea of depth, of development, and truth (Best and Kellner 1997: 174). This focus on style became very popular with Generation X until eventually stylistic traits associated with *avant-garde* postmodernism were co-opted by mainstream cinema as in, for example, films such as *Fight Club* (1999) by David Fincher or one of several by Christopher Nolan. In the early 1990s, however, Andrew Goodwin was able to observe that

> one of the most bizarre developments in the brief history of media and cultural studies is the way that abstruse French theory has 'trickled down' into the popular consciousness [...] so that the word 'postmodern' reached record stores, magazines, and television programs just a few years after it entered the academy.
>
> (Goodwin 1991: 186)

Postmodernism, then, was not simply the preserve of the academic but had wider currency in certain subcultures.

However, on the other hand, one of the key cultural preoccupations for Generation X – and particularly for those in certain subcultures – was *authenticity*. This notion sits somewhat uncomfortably with the idea that American culture uniformly endorses a kind of radical subjectivity where even the idea of truth is a grand narrative, and everyone is perfectly content to play ironically with free-floating images that have no substance. Indeed, how could one be authentic in a world where 'the real' was just another linguistic construct? The subcultural obsession with 'selling out' implied that there was, in the first place, something beyond the surface, something with genuine value that could be betrayed for financial gain. Dan Leidl suggests that Generation X came of age 'in a culture of dualism and irony, a world shrouded in surrealism yet emblazoned in hyper-authenticity' (Leidl 2013: xiii). *Clerks*, as with many other aspects of Generation X youth culture, wore its authenticity on its sleeve.

Clerks, Generation X, and 'indie'

One way to further understand this issue is to examine changes in American music across the second half of the twentieth century, particularly changes in the world of rock music. As the 1960s gave way to the 1970s and the era of Woodstock and Progressive Rock passed, by the mid-1970s rock music had veered towards two extremes. On the one hand, there was punk, notably contrasting with a hedonistic and often radio-friendly brand of hard rock on the other. This latter category would dominate the mainstream of American rock music until the late 1980s when a rougher, more inward-looking sound (with strong punk influences) would lead to a fundamental change. To understand this paradigm shift in American culture, one can borrow Joshua Clover's invocation of Raymond Williams' 'structures of feeling' to explain the explosion in popularity of grunge music in the early 1990s. In the 1980s, the 'dominant,' to use Williams' phrase (1977: 121), can be characterised as glam metal, hair metal, or one of many other (often derogatory) names by which this genre is known. This style of rock music is illustrated by the bestselling rock albums of the decade – Guns n' Roses' *Appetite for Destruction* (1987), Bon Jovi's *Slippery When Wet* (1986), *Hysteria* (1987) by Def Leppard, as well as other albums by these bands. Other well-known acts of this ilk such as Van Halen, Journey, and REO Speedwagon all sold records in large quantities. Taken together, this genre often demonstrated technical virtuosity, on the one hand, while combining this with a popular, accessible sensibility. Visually, the style tends towards excess, with the liberal use of make-up and costumes commonplace in bands like Mötley Crue and KISS, while stylised long hair was ubiquitous. To put it simply, the dominant convention of the 1980s is that a rock star is larger-than-life, and there is no mistaking a Gene Simmons or Slash for the boy next door (Clover 2009: 5–6).

By the late 1980s an alternative to mainstream rock was developing, one that rejected this level of obvious artifice. The shift towards alternative forms of rock music (and, most famously, grunge) in this period reflects, at some level, a similar movement in British culture in the 1970s. Dick Hebdige suggests that 'the punk aesthetic [was] formulated in the widening gap between artist and audience [and] can be read as an attempt to expose glam rock's contradictions' (Hebdige 1979: 63). Indeed, in a feature after Kurt Cobain's death, a writer for *Guitar World* magazine explains that while a British audience might struggle to find the novelty in Nirvana's rage-inspired, punk-infused brand of heavy metal, it comes partly because punk never gained the same mainstream presence in the US (Freedland 1994).

Whatever the musical debts of grunge might be, as a subculture, this phase of alternative rock music stands apart from punk in some key respects. Hebdige talks of the irony inherent in the fashions of punk and its connection with glam rock, even as it critiques those very styles. By contrast, the American alternative rock scene of the late 1980s and 1990s eschews this kind of ostentatious fashion. In place of chains and safety pins, grunge's most famous sartorial signifier is the comfortable flannel shirt, part of what Rick Marin once referred to as 'the Pacific Northwest's thrift-shop esthetic' (Marin 1992). Daniel Delis Hill writes that this style was 'a reaction to the elitist eighties. The affluence of Microsoft and Boeing employees was a conspicuous contrast to the mostly working-class population of the region' (Hill 2007: 136).

This style is particularly evident in *Clerks*. Though the black-and-white stock makes it difficult to declare authoritatively that the characters abjure the garish colours associated with punk, it appears that both Dante and Randal wear denim or check shirts throughout, in what might be called the unofficial uniform of the grunge rock fan. Bourdieu writes that

> The interest the different classes have in self-presentation, the attention they devote to it, their awareness of the profits it gives and the investment of time, effort, sacrifice and care which they actually put into it are proportionate to the chance of material or symbolic profit they can reasonably expect from it.
>
> (Bourdieu 1994: 202)

Following this thought, there is a straightforward connection between the grunge fans' pessimistic outlook on their generational prospects and the way that they dress. Far from the challenge to the status quo of punk, grunge's mode of resistance takes the form of withdrawal (see Figure 1.1).

Another key difference between punk and grunge is that the focus of the music is more likely to be the self than the social. While punk music tended to make overt political statements, in grunge the tendency is towards social alienation or other problems of the individual. It is this shift in focus that has led to accusations of narcissism, including the comment in a revealing piece by Jonathan Freedland following Cobain's death that 'it was also grimly appropriate that the boy-prince of the brat generation should die complaining of a tummy ache' (Freedland 1994). The truth is somewhat more nuanced: Cobain and other grunge acts such as Pearl Jam were vocal about sexism and eschewed what they saw as problematic aspects of 1980s

Figure 1.1 Dante Hicks and Randal Graves in clothing typical of their subculture.

rock star culture. Their perceived apoliticism came about solely because they were doing politics *differently*. In this, one might find yet another parallel with the world of independent film, a style that engages in politics in broadly the same way, since 'the emphasis has been on the small, local truth, as the film maker sees it, rather than the big stories and ideologies' (Davies and Wells 2002: 137).

This interrelation between various discourses of independence reaches its zenith in the film *Singles* (Crowe, 1992). This romantic comedy focuses on characters from the Generation X demographic, though it is perhaps more famous for being embedded within the grunge subculture, and is 'a prominent example of a Hollywood depiction of indie music subculture' (Sexton 2017: 113). Despite its release by a major label and its production through the help of a substantial budget, *Singles* was able to tap into enough of a subcultural cachet to blur the lines between Hollywood and indie cinema and achieve a kind of credibility with youth audiences. The soundtrack to the movie featured grunge royalty such as Pearl Jam, Soundgarden, and Alice in Chains, while the fictional band in the movie (of which actor Matt Dillon's character was a member) also featured members of Pearl Jam. Moreover, grunge is a subgenre of music that offers us a useful way into thinking about some of these issues, since its associations with social change have resulted in more theorisation than other music subgenres in volumes such as Ryan Moore's *Sells Like Teen Spirit* (2010) and Catherine Strong's *Grunge: Music and Memory* (2017). This increased theoretical interest has related to both the music itself and the wider the social factors that surround it.

However, though it offers us a point of departure, it is important to remember that not all alternative rock music aligns with grunge. For one thing, the ensuing analysis of *Clerks* will make clear that very little of the music featured on the film's soundtrack fits comfortably within the grunge framework, with a notable exception being the inclusion of 'Got Me Wrong' by Alice in Chains. Despite this, the film's soundtrack is more of an amalgam of different influences in contemporary alternative rock music at this point in history. A second and still more important reason, as far as the present volume is concerned, is that many of these discourses that have been outlined as relevant to grunge apply more broadly to alternative rock music.

Given the chapter's focus on indie cinema, it is convenient that an entire genre of music exists with the same handle. Though it means crossing the Atlantic, Wendy Fonarow's research into British indie music can be instructive here. In a comment that reflects the difficulty in defining American independent cinema, Fonarow writes 'Fans and members of the British music industry often struggle to come to terms with defining something that they feel they can recognize intuitively' (Fonarow 2006: 25). As with indie cinema, no definition of indie music seems to fit the bill, either including artists who should be excluded or excluding those who belong within that camp by common consensus. However, despite a seeming inability to fix the meaning of indie, to stabilise the concept, it is still used in various ways that reveal the values of the subculture. Indeed, it is the distinction of the subculture from the mainstream that is at the heart of such processes of definition:

> an attempt at self-definition is part of the process of forming a cultural grouping. To form a group, members need to create a set of boundaries between what constitutes and what excludes membership. Creating a boundary means creating an identity for yourself.
>
> (Fonarow 2006: 25–6)

This work highlights that one of the most important philosophical concerns when defining indie music is something introduced earlier in this chapter: the idea of authenticity. Assuming that there is some notion of 'genuine' music, indie argues that artists only produce this at a distance from the generic output of major music corporations. Fonarow links this explicitly to centuries-old debates around religion, arguing that 'indie's core values promote and replicate the doctrine of a particular brand of Protestant religiosity: Puritanism,' while still recognising that it is unlikely that the indie culture itself would recognise its attitudes as consistent with such a label (Fonarow 2006: 28). In this instance, purity relates not so much to a true relation with the divine but to the essence of music itself, with the argument being that the institutional machinery surrounding the music industry in the modern corporate environment is so great that genuine connection is only possible outside those stultifying environs. In the call for a return to something more 'authentic,' indie music – and its preoccupation with a closer relationship between performer and audience – offers a restatement of the Punk DIY movement. If this seems at odds with the pure postmodernism sometimes associated with this period, again, one should not be surprised: the fascination with authenticity and the desire to reclaim something 'genuine' from the past is a common alternative reaction to late capitalism.

There is no reason to suppose that such impulses are unique to British indie music, either. The American scholar Sarah Thornton has identified very similar inclinations in a youth subculture at some remove from the world of rock, namely that of club and rave cultures. At some level, this is a surprise: the two groups are often seen as opposites, not least of all by each other. As Thornton suggests, 'rock criticism and much pop scholarship have tended to privilege "listening" over dance music, visibly performing musicians over behind-the-scenes producers, the rhetorically "live" over the "recorded" and hence guitars over synthesizers and samplers' (Thornton 1996 :1–2). Rock musicians and their fans have historically been likely to present themselves as if the experience is more esoteric than that of their electronic music counterparts. There is also the likelihood that rock subcultures see dance music as an extension of mindless pop, banal at its best and an instance of mass and popular culture at its worst. Some rock fans might be shocked to learn, then, that there are hierarchies within dance music. Moreover, the latter subculture is still more youth-oriented given the typical age range at which one might frequent nightclubs and raves regularly, and members of that cultural group often talk about dance music using similar vocabulary and assumptions as other, more traditionally respected genres. Indeed, the mysterious cult of listening so central to rock music is displaced here by an equally obscure cult of *feeling*. Even dissimilar youth cultures, then, operate around a shared idea of being distinct in some way. It is unsurprising, then, that beyond these similarities Thornton identifies repeated references in discourses of dance cultures to an us-and-them dynamic and allusions to an imagined homogeneous mainstream that the subculture is defined against:

> This contrast between 'us' and the 'mainstream' is more directly related to the process of envisioning social worlds and discriminating between social groups. Its veiled elitism and separatism enlist and reaffirm binary oppositions such as the alternative and the straight, the diverse and the homogeneous, the radical and the conformist, the distinguished and the common. The mainstream is a trope which, once prised open,

reveals the complex and cryptic relations between age and the social structure.

(Thornton 1996: 5)

Though the subcultures surrounding these genres are usually seen as opposites, what links them with each other – and, indeed, with American youth cultures, including grunge – is how they all present themselves in opposition to the majority. The problem with the mainstream (as formulated by these groups) is that it is the antithesis of authentic culture. Quite what that authentic culture 'is' always evades exact definition, but the one thing that is consistent is that it is considered by these groups as incompatible with the contemporary systems of capitalism that govern our everyday lives. Whatever it is, it cannot be marketed to 'us' in the same way that 'we' might buy cereal or other everyday commodities. Thornton continues:

> The idea that authentic culture is somehow outside media and commerce is a resilient one. In its full-blown romantic form, the belief suggests that grassroots cultures resist and struggle with a colonizing mass-mediated corporate world. At other times, the perspective lurks between the lines, inconspicuously informing parameters of research, definitions and culture and judgements of value.
>
> (Thornton 1996: 116)

It seems a familiar stance to fall back on this ill-defined idea of authenticity, and it is observable in justifications for the existence of independent cinema, as well as repeatedly in other subcultures. It stands, then, as a crucial tenet in several cultural strains. Furthermore, as noted with the above reference to grunge, this attitude is predictably not limited to these British subgenres of music but runs throughout the kinds of American alternative rock that fill the soundtrack for *Clerks*. To branch out from the soundtrack for a moment to a song that demonstrates related views, one might consider the 1985 song 'We Care A Lot,' by the band Faith No More. It was released on an independent label, Mordam Records, but perhaps more critical to its status with alternative crowds is the tone and subject matter of the song. The lyrics parody the earnestness of 1980s pop stars and charitable movements such as Live Aid. As well as being a volley towards the most visible manifestations of the corporate music mainstream, one can identify in this a bearing towards philanthropy. The song seems to imply that it is better to be genuine in one's sentiments and do nothing than to contribute to a common cause solely because it is something others deem worthy. Here, we are at a great distance from a virtue theory of ethics and sit far more comfortably with an existentialist view of the world.

That the soundtrack to *Clerks* is made up exclusively with this kind of alternative rock music is no coincidence, and if one wants to comprehend this film, its significance should not be downplayed. Featuring a mixture of punk and alternative rock acts signed to independent labels along with local, relatively unknown bands (with only a few exceptions including the aforementioned Alice in Chains and Soul Asylum, who were both signed to Columbia at that point), this soundtrack is no mere backdrop to the film but indissolubly linked with the images on screen. An instance of this is the sequence early in the film in which we see Dante getting ready to go in after being called into work. Here, we see him dressing in the appropriate clothing of this subgroup while the images onscreen are overlaid by the band Love Among Freaks, a local (New Jersey) outfit that plays a brash style of rock music which fits with the film's lo-fi, somewhat rebellious aesthetic. The aural qualities of this film, then, connote not just independence, but a specific *type* of independence, one linked to an existing subculture that has its own values, interests, and philosophical touchstones.

Within this subculture, independence is something of a Romantic notion. Freedom to be one's true self is all-important, though it is only possible by removing oneself from coercive forces in society as much as possible. In music, this often manifests itself in staying clear of the mainstream music industry entirely, 'with indie label musicians who moved on from indie labels to major labels often accused by their fans of "selling out"' (Shuker 2017: 185). Sexton observes that this extends beyond music, and that *Singles* was criticised by some in the subculture for a perceived inauthenticity: it was 'apparently hated by Kurt Cobain, [and] it was dismissed by Kaya Oakes [...] as an example of the co-optation of indie in the early 1990s and, in her words, "was enough to make an indie musician puke"' (Sexton 2017: 114). Major labels and productions that reflected their greater budgets were suspect. Independent records and films might be comparatively cheaply produced and consequently rough around the edges, but that very lack of polish became a signifier of independence from corporate interference and of authenticity.

When these factors are considered, *Clerks* exists not as a free-floating cinematic artefact but as something grounded in the ideological conditions of its day, one that is necessarily figured by (and through) a matrix of related discourses around what it means to be 'alternative' or 'independent.' These discourses reflect the values of a distinct youth culture, and there is consequently a sense of belonging imbued by the film. Authenticity is always a problematic notion when it comes to cinema, and the interesting contradictions raised by the Miramax connection have already been addressed. And there is further need to be careful: Thornton reminds her readers that 'inconsistent fantasies of the mainstream are rampant in subcultural studies. They are probably the single most important reason why subsequent cultural studies find pockets of symbolic resistance wherever they look' (Thornton 1996: 93). There is a need to take care in any study like this to ensure that one does not project one's own sense of resistance onto the text, to find subversion where none convincingly exists. Nevertheless, the combination of the style, of Smith's unusual story (complete with Romantic, 'exceptional man' creator overtone), the film's attitude towards other cinematic and visual art forms, and its use of music that fits in with a particular group's notion of 'real' music all lead to it occupying a distinctive place in its zeitgeist. *Clerks* is a particularly emblematic film, one seen as being produced *by* a member of a particular group of young people *for* the members of that group. Throughout the remainder of this book, it will be apparent how the attitudes of that group towards employment, consumption, sex, and masculinity all necessarily inform their treatment in the film.

2   'A job that makes a difference'

Youth and employment

The portrait of Generation X as a group that had a chip on their collective shoulder is valid, but equally, a look at the economic landscape through the 1970s and 1980s suggests that it might not be without good cause. Their parents had been a generation raised on the relative prosperity of the post-war period. The United States was not only enjoying its status as a Superpower on the world stage but was also a wealthy country at this point. A creditor during the Second World War, the country had started receiving payments in peacetime. Of still more significance in the post-war economic boom was the redistribution of wartime resources, as industrial resources that had been channelled towards the war effort were directed *en masse* to the production of consumer goods after the conflict. As a result, the 1950s was a decade in which televisions, refrigerators, and other household goods all became much more readily available to the average American, and as a result, jobs were relatively abundant both in the manufacture and selling of these items.

Of course, there is a need to not overinflate such claims. As much as this was a society in which consumer culture flourished, it was the same society of which Michael Harrington could subsequently write of an 'other America,' one where 'tens of millions of Americans are, at this very moment, maimed in body and spirit, existing at levels beneath those necessary for human decency' (Harrington 1997: 2). When one speaks of the general prosperity of the period, that does not remove the fact that there were millions untouched by that increase in fortunes. Sadly, though, this disparity is something that recurs throughout US history, and so without wishing to downplay the continuing economic straits of many millions, it is still accurate to say that, relatively speaking at least, the parents of Generation X generally matured in economic conditions that led to optimism, despite violent clashes over Civil Rights, the well-documented growth in therapy culture, and the rise of a counterculture that would lead to the Woodstock festival and widespread protests against the war in Vietnam.

Their offspring, however, would have a quite different experience. From the time that they were born to the point where they were looking to enter the workforce, there were rapid changes in American demographics and employment prospects. These shifts cut the ground out from under their feet and saw optimism for the future replaced with an apathetic, resigned pessimism. First, there was a rapid transfer from urban to suburban living with a move from a mostly industrial workforce to one based more in the office than the factory. As Brian Jarvis put it:

> In 1950, over 70 per cent of Americans lived in cities, 30 per cent of the labour force was employed in manufacturing and the industrial regions of the Northeast and the Midwest were on the verge of an economic boom. By 1980 this economic landscape was to be transformed beyond recognition. Factories and the city were displaced by offices and the suburbs as an American's most familiar geographical experience.
>
> (Jarvis 1998: 13)

This transformation was compounded when, during the 1980s, the US, like several other major economies, would experience significant deindustrialisation, leading to many jobs in this sector being replaced by those in the service industry. A repeated complaint of the Reagan economic revolution is that the quality of jobs available was not as high as it had been in the previous generation. From this perspective, the composition of the market was skewed more and more in favour of the corporations that employed people at the expense of those performing the tasks. Youth culture of the period often presents an attitude to employment prospects that recalls Thorstein Veblen's expressed comment of 'our habitual aversion to menial employments' (Veblen 1994: 8). For the first time in generations, Americans did not believe that the future would be better than it had been for their parents, an attitude that manifests in apathy towards the central institutions that some young people saw as intractable. During this period, young people in America can almost be said to be *doubly* alienated – not just in the Marxist sense in that their relation to their labour is abstracted but alienated over and above that by the abstraction of the very *reason* for which they sell their labour in the first place.

This moment, then, is a crucial point at which economics intersects with (and, indeed, partially shapes) the aesthetic and philosophical underpinnings of this subculture. When Kurt Cobain died in 1994, the *Guardian* journalist Jonathan Freedland travelled to Seattle, the epicentre of the grunge movement, to report on the reaction. While there, Freedland talked to many of the Generation Xers who were fans of the band's music. From reflections on the idea that grunge itself was already over, commoditised beyond its conceptual limits once it proved to have market value, to Cobain's role as a reluctant hero who wore his fame uncomfortably, the article communicates that those attracted to Nirvana experienced a sense of futility about their employment prospects. Freedland quotes one twenty-six-year-old, 'who has completed six years of study in molecular biology but is now heading for Alaska to work as a salmon fisherman' (Freedland 1994). He goes on to talk of the anger that comes from not knowing what to do or what one is supposed to be and that comes from feeling as if there is no way of exerting any control over the future. Whatever one chooses, life offers nothing more than a diet of monotony. In the same article, Freedland talks to another person in the famous Crocodile Café who 'despite a college degree is working as a postman – a textbook case of the X syndrome which has overeducated kids working in low-status, low-paid jobs, from office temps to despatch riders.' For critics such as Jarvis, this reorganisation of the labour market is a direct result of government policy:

> Since the monopolisation of political power by the New Right in North America and the UK in the 1980s, there has been a degree of convergence between governmental economic policies and visions of the postindustrial future. Reaganism, Thatcherism and (to a lesser extent) their successors have involved economic strategies entirely consonant with the imperatives of the global village and the information city. For example, in both rhetoric and practice, western governments and multinational corporations have used variations on this thesis to legitimate the 'shedding' (a favourite naturalising metaphor) of jobs in the manufacturing sector.
>
> (Jarvis 1998: 28)

In this framework, the neoliberal policies that dominated right-wing politics in the US (and, as Jarvis indicates, the UK) exacerbated several postmodern trends. This agenda contributed to many well-paying jobs leaving more economically developed countries in favour of nations and geographical territories where labour could be purchased relatively inexpensively.

As it became clear by the late 1980s that many Gen Xers could only find work in low-paying jobs (seen by many as low-skill), articles began to appear in the press questioning the proliferation of what became known as 'McJobs.' This phrase seems to have begun its life in a *Washington Post* story that argued that working in the fast food industry harmed those in high school since those jobs imparted few skills that would be useful later in life and had an impact on school attendance (Etzioni 1986). From there, though, the term developed to take on a broader sense that the inevitable conclusion of 'Reaganomics' was that, though the unemployment rate was dropping, the young could only work in jobs that would offer them a future decidedly less rosy than that of their parents. The fundamental question concerned whether it was the quantity or the quality of available work that was more important.

This economic dilemma was debated in the press through the mid to late 1980s. Articles such as those in the *New York Times* which claimed that 'the collapse of America's basic industries is throwing off far more blue-collar workers than can be reabsorbed into other high-paying jobs, even during the recent years of record growth' (Reich 1985) would be countered by those in the *Washington Post* that stated

> in truth, manufacturing and services need each other. These are not competing functions. Remember, the industrial sector isn't shrinking, except as *percentage* of the work force, and that's not because it's getting smaller (it isn't) but because of the incredible boom in the service sector.
>
> (Brock 1987)

This second quotation is taken from an article in the *Post* written by Bill Brock, Reagan's Secretary of Labor, and it drew a rebuttal in the same paper from Democratic congressman Augustus F. Hawkins. The latter said that Brock's piece 'served as a wonderful reminder that the Reagan campaign is hard at work preparing for another presidential campaign' and contradicted this rosy vision of the economy, stating 'the growth in service jobs is not the real issue […] unfortunately it takes two new service jobs to equal the wages of one lost in manufacturing' (Hawkins 1987). Other influential publications, such as the explicitly conservative *National Review*, also took a predictably hard-line position in their own examination of the issue, with the *Review* essentially arguing that the situation was invented and claiming that, for political purposes, the Democratic Party had 'to turn obvious wealth into illusory poverty' ('The Myth of "McJobs"' 1987: 19).

It is not the purpose of this volume to assess the merits of these claims. Whatever the economic reality during these debates in the 1980s, it was clear that the prosperity of the US was not to last. Fiscal necessity forced George H.W. Bush to renege on a campaign pledge to issue no new taxes, a decision that many call a significant contribution to his loss in the 1992 Presidential election. By the time Bill Clinton took office in 1993, the economic situation seemed so dire that all other concerns were made subordinate to this sobering reality. According to Bob Woodward's account of the first year of the Clinton presidency, at this time 'all of the campaign promises […] had to be reevaluated in the context of the new economic situation they faced. The group [Clinton's team] had to step back and ask: what were their goals? What was possible?' (Woodward 1994: 81). This contraction, then, is the economic backdrop from the middle of the Reagan presidency, through his successor, and into the first years of the Clinton administration, when *Clerks* was made. Such a downturn in American fortunes, following on from a period in which the 'boom' was *itself* a contested idea of debatable benefit to the average American, would necessarily leave its imprint on American culture.

'McJobs' in American culture

Regardless of any individual political persuasion, one thing is clear: that the ideas that the economy forced people to work in 'McJobs' and that the country was seeing the prospects for the average American dwindle had both entered the *zeitgeist* by the time Freedland interviewed those Seattle-based grunge fans in the wake of Cobain's suicide. If there is one person more responsible for articulating this, it is perhaps the writer now most associated with the word 'McJob,' the Canadian author Douglas Coupland, who popularised the term in his 1991 novel *Generation X: Tales of an Accelerated Culture*. A few months before *Clerks* was released, a feature in the *New York Times* reported that 'Three years after it was published by St. Martin's Press, it is still selling nearly 6,000 copies a month, and more than 300,000 copies are in print' (Lohr 1994). That same year, John Fraser of *Saturday Night* wrote of Coupland that

> In the States, he's cruising around in guru stratosphere: the Jack Kerouac of his generation (the post-boomer generation of disaffected techno-punks who don't know the words to either 'God Save the Queen' or 'O Canada'), a new-minted McLuhan, Homer to the microserfs. He's been on the cover of *Wired*. The op-ed page of *The New York Times* uses him when it tries to appear mod and rad.
>
> (Fraser 1994: 8)

Despite being a relatively weak seller in its early months and having a troubled publication history that saw the book rejected by its Canadian publisher (when Coupland delivered a novel rather than the non-fiction book he was contracted to write), *Generation X* achieved both popularity with its target audience and a similar status in the nation's imaginary as films such as *Slacker* that were released around the same time. In fact,

> Coupland recounts how his novel received no attention when it first hit bookstores in March 1991. It wasn't until the grunge music explosion in Seattle and the release of Richard Linklater's film *Slacker* (1990)

that 'Generation X' (along with 'slacker' and 'grunge') became 'buzzwords' for the younger generation.

(Tropiano 2006: 217)

Again, one can observe a cultural moment in which shared interests manifest across diverse instances of youth film, literature, and music.

Like the films of this period already mentioned, *Generation X* displays a sense of irony that tends towards nihilism, as well as the kind of generational consciousness that the title itself naturally suggests. However, perhaps the most notable stylistic feature of *Generation X* is the inclusion of a series of explanatory notes at the bottom of many pages. These offer definitions of the slang terms used in the book and given 'the change from non-fiction to fiction, most reviewers viewed the marginalia and appendix of the book as remnants of the non-fiction intention' (Doody 2011: 13–14). For the purposes of this chapter, it is worthwhile to take a moment to include Coupland's note that describes the term 'McJob': 'A low-pay, low-prestige, low-dignity, low-benefit, no-future job in the service sector. Frequently considered a satisfying career choice by people who have never held one' (Coupland 1991: 6). This reference to the dignity (or lack of it) in the jobs that one performs brings to mind not only Veblen's judgement about people's innate aversion to menial employment but also David Riesman's observation regarding 'the feeling of shame in not having a job that is involved' (Riesman 1993: 169). Further afield, Jean Baudrillard expressed a similar idea rather more extravagantly when he lamented that 'today all labour falls under a single definition, that bastard, archaic and unanalysed category of service-labour, and not the supposedly universal classical definition of "proletarian" wage-labour' (Baudrillard 2017: 39). A brief moment in the film *Singles* that expresses this shame or confusion occurs when Cliff (Matt Dillon) observes that in his role as the delivery person for a florist, the next day he will have to sneak into someone's apartment and spell out the occupier's name in rose petals. He asks, incredulously, 'Do you believe this job?'

Each of the philosophers mentioned in the previous paragraph was writing before the term McJob had been coined, but there are identifiable traces of their philosophies in how Generation X used the word during the 1980s and early 1990s. As the 1980s came to an end, a term which had been used in the news media was given particular definition and a new cultural lease of life through its centrality to a work of fiction, one that had significant importance for the very generation that actually had to work in the type of employment that was, for the commentators, a matter of mere theory. In the aforementioned piece on Coupland, Fraser writes that

> Doug was going to go undercover at a McDonald's restaurant. He would stay there until he was either fired or named employee-of-the-month – whichever came first. Genius that he is, instead of doing it he identified 'McJobs' as the highest sort of employment many members of his turned-off, cynical generation would be able to attain, and astutely left the grunt work of serving the fries to others.
>
> (Fraser 1994: 8)

The telling point here is that the reaction against McJobs in *Generation X* is because they are the best that many members of Coupland's generation are going to be able to hope for. Rather than a way into the workforce before progressing to something with better long-term prospects, the McJob has become an end-in-itself. Consequently, Coupland's novel lashes out at the world created by late capitalism in which people must work harder, in less fulfilling jobs, while still earning and achieving less than their predecessors, all while being considered inferior by that same privileged generation.

Beyond the more material aspects, such as the feeling that one was working in order to gain less and that American prospects were going backwards, the reason that McJobs present such a problem in *Generation X* is that the notion of the human subject in the text is inherently Romantic. As Wing-Chi Ki suggests, the central characters in the novel

> favor an honest, heart-oriented Rousseauistic community. Their rationale for rejecting the urban world is not unlike Rousseau's hatred against the way people practice deception, consumption and luxury in the city. If Dag (one of the characters in *Generation X*) calls these people 'Dickoid' (25), Coleridge would consider them to be 'prostituted genius' for they have 'ever-shifting perspective' to offer to the 'vanity of youth.'
>
> (Ki 2003: 16)

In one sense, then, although Generation X was thought a particularly modern phenomenon, the guiding principles of the group came from centuries earlier, in the form of a Romantic philosophy of the self. Bernard Rosenthal writes that

> out of the vast quantity of critical study on American Romanticism, agreement has emerged on at least one point: American Romantics experienced a conflict between themselves and the culture within which they lived, between the myth they sought to create and the historical world in which they were 'implicated.'
>
> (Rosenthal 1980: 16)

In their discomfort with the society that existed around them, then, the subcultures of Generation X may indeed have been just the latest in a long line of American Romantics.

Equally, artworks about such characters and their connections to the world of employment are not necessarily a particularly modern invention, either. Those with a knowledge of the American literary canon might anticipate the invocation of Herman Melville's Bartleby, a character with shades of transcendentalism, who is 'private, intense, ensnared by his own purity' (Davis 2018: 498). Bartleby's repeated assertion that he 'would prefer not to' perform any of the tasks associated with his job or fit in with any of the expectations of society that conflict with his understanding of his soul led inexorably to his downfall. Melville wrote 'Bartleby, The Scrivener' in part as a satire of transcendentalist philosophy (cf. Sten 1974), and Bartleby cannot be true to himself and survive in the world – a dilemma with which the characters in Coupland's *Generation X* might well sympathise. Transcendentalism might be a distinctly American philosophy, but Melville's text calls into question its practicality for the average American citizen. Michael Gilmore neatly summarises this profound social dimension of the story for us with his observation that '"Bartleby" is a story about America, and its tragedy is American' (Gilmore 2010: 143).

The critical difference between these early versions of Romanticism and those we encounter in the late twentieth century is that the modern world has largely eroded ideas of the transcendental or of the divine. If one can only achieve something with truth by escaping the social or the corporate, the question remains, where can one even escape *to* in our all-encompassing society? Though Bartleby did not escape, American culture is full of characters who have attempted to push on to new frontiers or locations. Susan Field gives us some examples of this from classic American literature, noting that

> When a romance hero cannot recognize himself, or cannot be recognized by others for who he is, the time for the journey out has arrived. Some heroes, like Melville's Ishmael, set sail, whereas some, like Twain's Huckleberry Finn, light out for new territory.
>
> (Field 1997: 7)

Closer to the time of *Clerks*, beatnik and hippie culture had both produced subcultures that seemed to opt out of society in addition to their more popular, less radical iterations, and Ronald Primeau writes of the Romanticism that comes out of the road narratives of this period (Primeau 1996).

However, for Generation X, no such escape is possible in American culture, neither geographically nor ideologically. There is no sustained belief that meaning can be found in any alternative to the cycle of capitalism and consumerism. Much as grunge had been co-opted by major record labels once there was a clear financial incentive to capitalise on this subculture, Coupland's would-be hermits are necessarily bound by the world that has created them. Unable to think beyond the information overload imposed on them since their infancy, all they can do is reproduce signs from previous decades, obscure references to popular culture in ever more ironised versions. It is perhaps telling that around the time that Coupland was writing *Generation X*, a character in *Slacker* asks 'Who's ever written the great work about the immense effort required [...] in order not to create? Intensity without mastery. The obsessiveness of the utterly passive.' Here, the Romantic position of the creative artistic type is redrawn and reoriented around the withdrawn attitudes of this new generation.

Employment in *Clerks*

Clerks does not replicate these older ideas in such a blatant fashion. There is no clear retreat from the world, no 'lighting out for the territory,' in the way that we might find in any number of significant American texts from Henry David Thoreau to Jack Kerouac. This film is set almost entirely within the workplace, and so, by definition, it does not (indeed, *can*not) involve a literal withdrawal from that environment. With that said, the Romantic frames evident elsewhere can still be found in the film, albeit in a far more implicit form. The balance between the demands of the world of employment and the spirit of the individual subject is still of vital importance to the film's underlying rationale. In this, *Clerks* and *Generation X* share many discursive strains common to the youth subcultures of the 1980s and 1990s. It is for this reason that Hanson writes that '*Clerks* [...] is among the most vivid illustrations of young people stuck in dead-end jobs' (Hanson 2002: 79). The attitude to work is probably best summarised in the last action before the second chapter title slide, in which Dante, having run through his preparatory work and taking his place behind the desk, puts his head down on it, in a move approaching despair. Within this Romantic structure, this kind of work might best be described as 'soul-crushing.'

Why is this workplace the cause of such misery in the first place? In truth, Dante has several relationships forced upon him through working in the convenience store, and these are often the source of his grievances. Perhaps the most fundamental is with his employer, a relationship that essentially acts as the catalyst for all subsequent events. The film begins with his manager calling Dante into work on what is supposed to be his day off. The first sound we hear is the phone ringing, when Dante, nowhere to be seen in the first few shots, falls out of the closet, presumably after a night of such heavy partying that he could not find his bed. Even at this stage, we still do not see his face as he lies prostrate on the floor while on the phone. The audience is only allowed to hear one half of the conversation, but it is clear that Dante does not want to come into work. He offers excuses, such as his being 'tired,' he is 'playing hockey at two,' and that he 'just closed last night,' and his suggestion that they try calling Randal instead. The way he communicates, whining excuses rather than declaring his intentions with more firmness, suggests there is something submissive about Dante, and it is not a surprise when ultimately, none of these strategies is successful (Soles 2008: 13).

Dante's last-ditch strategy is to make a bargain, based on when the boss will be able to relieve him: he elicits a promise that the store owner will be there by twelve, or he will not come in at all, before struggling to put the phone down while still lying on the floor. Around forty minutes into the film, Dante finds out that contrary to their agreement, his boss has no intention of showing up. The scene plays out as a betrayal: the young clerk is disbelieving and incredulous when he finds out that his boss has taken a trip to Vermont for several days and so clearly *never* had any intention of honouring their agreement. This perfidy is compounded when Dante learns of it not from his boss but from his mother, who calls the store (how she knows is not revealed to us). Nevertheless, what is evident here is a notable contempt for the young people who work in these jobs by their superiors, the very people who should think enough of the job to do it properly. Dante's boss simply assumes that, having little-to-no career option besides the store, Dante will cover for him despite his plans and their agreement to the contrary. This exchange, of which we only ever see Dante's half, and which takes but little screen time, is the prime generational conflict of the film.

On arrival at the store, one of Dante's first tasks is to create a banner stating that the store really is open, because the security shutters have been jammed since someone forced chewing gum into the lock (see Figure 2.1). This vandalism is, on the one hand, just an additional irritant for Dante, but it is also evidence of a deeper trend running throughout the film. Everywhere we look, this is a world in a state of decay. A pivotal moment in the plot occurs primarily because the lights in the convenience store stop working 'at 5.14 every day' for reasons that Randal – who is minding the store at the time – is unable to explain. Crucially, though, he knows that their boss will not pay to fix them because the electrician owes money to the video store. While Randal may not know the cause of the problem, he is all too aware of the social and economic factors that explain why they have not been solved by those with the power to do so.

Randal is the second primary character in *Clerks* and works in the video store next door. In many ways, he is the opposite of Dante. Both, though,

Figure 2.1 Dante puts up his makeshift sign.

are young characters who belong to the same youth subculture, and so despite differences in philosophy and outlook, they have a generational link that binds them together. We anticipate Randal before we ever see him on screen: reference is made to him before his arrival (long after the store's stated opening hours). On his first appearance he pretends to be a customer in order to make a bet with another customer of the video store that she will not be able to rent a particular tape – a bet which, as the clerk of the store, he will necessarily win. He immediately heads into the convenience store and sees Dante and tells him that 'if I knew you were here, I'd have come even later.' This attitude, both in general and to his work more specifically, will run throughout Randal's exchanges with everyone in the film.

The absence of the employer in question means that whatever the significance of that generational conflict – and one can still read a lot into this relationship despite the absence of one party – one must look elsewhere in order to see this conflict manifest more fully on-screen. This antagonism plays out not with those who employ the clerks, but those who *buy* from them, and the film 'pulses with anger at the inanity of what people have to do for a living. The two clerks in the movie [...] ooze contempt for their customers because their customers, intentionally or not, ooze contempt for them' (Hanson 2002: 79). Throughout the film, Dante must serve customers who are entitled or needy. In a scene that will be discussed in more detail in the third chapter, Dante is harassed by a whole group of customers for selling cigarettes, after which one of his harassers asks for a pack, which he disbelievingly slams down on the counter. One of the more unpleasant customers is the man waiting for Randal to arrive to open the video store, who is aggressive towards Dante because of his impatience. When Dante eventually snaps back, he replies 'go ahead. Crack wise. That's why you're jockeying a register in some fucking local convenience store instead of doing an honest day's work.' Implicit in this gesture is a downplaying of the importance of the service sector and the young people who fill those roles by the very people *using* those services.

The suggestion that this is somehow less honest than other forms of work plays to the Generation X anxiety about how worthwhile their jobs are. However, at the same time, it ignores the complicity of older generations, and the political establishment more broadly, in creating an economy based on a job profile that they, themselves, implicitly do not value, whatever the official political line may be. The film dramatises this in such a way that Dante can gain a victory that is not always available in less comic narratives, as we see him throw away the keys that this unpleasant customer had left on the counter in his haste. In many ways, this is the perfect Generation X riposte. This one act requires little effort and has done nothing to upset the overall balance of power or change Dante's situation, but it offers a posture of defiance nonetheless. We see the older man back looking for his keys at the front of the store where he meets Randal, perhaps the character least likely to assist, who quotes Short Round from *Indiana Jones and The Temple of Doom* (Spielberg, 1984) and passes on quickly.

Though this stands as perhaps the instance where hostility from a customer is at its most blatant, this is far from the only instance in *Clerks* where customers represent a nightmare scenario. In two of the most famous scenes in the film, customers both lead anti-smoking mobs and die in the staff bathroom (discussed more fully in Chapters 4 and 5, respectively). But aside from these key scenes, the film is rife with moments where customers demand more of the clerks than their job description implies. In one exchange, Dante helps a customer remove a tube of potato chips from the end of his arm (see Figure 2.2). The customer observes that he usually tips the end of the can up to get the last chips, but in this case, he has inexplicably decided to try and reach the final few, only to get his hand stuck. His revelation that he thought he might have to go to the hospital seems like a throwaway line but is instead deeply revealing as to just how much expectation is being placed on Dante. Though he is only paid minimum wage, he is at some small level standing in for a medical professional here, essentially giving the same service despite a vast deficit in training, experience, and perhaps most important of all, recompense. Of course, this might lead one to consider the importance of the cost of health care in the US, but whatever

Figure 2.2 Dante assists a customer.

the underlying cause, the effect is much the same on those forced to pick up the slack.

This last example is one of many in the film in which the customers in the store serve to acutely inconvenience – or worse, harass – Dante. If there is one thing that is common to both clerks' experience, it is a given that customers will do whatever the clerks do not expect or want. The film plays up this tendency to act in inconvenient ways for comic effect; most notably, when the protagonists are away from the store and Dante guiltily questions his absence, Randal asks him how often they ever have to serve people at this time of the day, on a Saturday. This is enough to convince Dante. From there, though, we immediately cut to a shot of the closed store door, with a veritable plague of customers impatiently banging on the door.

However, though Randal enjoys a similarly confrontational relationship with his customers, there is a noticeably different power dynamic at work in his interactions with them. This is largely a result of specific responses that mitigate the unpleasantness of the working environment, and as such they will be discussed in more detail in the next chapter. Nevertheless, there are a few points relevant to the context of this chapter and its focus on the 'no prospects' employment for the American youth in the 1990s. Randal pays so little attention that he wordlessly sells a packet of cigarettes to a child. Randal's attitude to his job is generally poor, though it is rare that his apathy leads directly to something quite so morally questionable. It is in keeping with the tone of the film that it is Dante, rather than Randal himself, who pays the consequence for this act, being cited later in the film after we learn that the girl's mother has complained to the authorities. Later in the film, a customer asks the name of a cat seen in the store on several occasions, to which Randal replies 'annoying customer.' After the customer swears at him and leaves, this prompts Dante to ask him to treat the customers better in future. Randal, naturally enough, ignores this and even escalates the displays of his antipathy when a few minutes later, he actively spits water in the face of yet another customer.

One of the main differences between this and several key Generation X texts is that Randal seems to take a limited form of ownership for his situation. In *Generation X* and *Slacker*, the narratives strongly imply that the organisation of social structures is such that there is little that the individual can do in reply. Despite being the philosopher of the film and the surest mouthpiece for the slacker generation, Randal sees things somewhat differently. He tells Dante, explicitly, that Dante needs to 'shit or get off the pot,' and that if he hates his job, he can work to change it. It becomes clear that Randal is not the Gen X figure we have seen elsewhere who acts like this because there he sees no alternative. His motive is that he likes the feeling of no responsibility, of being virtually free from pursuing anything more. He notes that what lies at the root of Dante staying where he is at is comfort – that quitting for another job would require significant effort and would threaten to shatter the illusion that he has fashioned for himself. In this, he reflects Douglas Coupland's definition of 'occupational slumming' from *Generation X*: 'Taking a job well beneath one's skill or education level as a means of retreat from adult responsibilities and/or avoiding possible failure in one's true occupation' (Coupland 1991: 130).

However, the film posits this as something that Dante does as an individual, rather than being an all-consuming social malaise that cannot be avoided. This trait is something internal to the character, who shares a story about his infancy and remarks 'the point is, I'm not the type of person who'll disrupt things just so I can shit comfortably.' When Randal finally loses his temper after hearing 'I'm not supposed to be here today' for what feels like the hundredth time, he snaps, telling Dante that it is *his* fault, that he is there of his own volition, and that he believes the store will fall apart if he is absent. Crucially, he tells him that 'you overcompensate for having what's basically a monkey's job.' His final verdict is damning, telling Dante that he is 'obsessed with making it more important, more epic than it is. You work in a convenience store, badly I might add.' At some level it is hard not to link Randal's position here with Smith's own efforts to change his situation by making *Clerks* in the first place. One might give still more weight to this when noticing that, on the commentary track for the DVD, Smith reveals that he originally cast himself in the role, only to decide it was too large a part to take on himself.[1]

38 'A job that makes a difference'

So far, this chapter has primarily focused on the employment that we see on screen, namely that of Dante and Randal. However, it would be a mistake to think that this is the sole extent to which the film deals with employment. This last rant from Randal is just part of a wider discourse of the world of work that allows the film to comment – with the irony inherent to a Gen X frame of mind – on the broader American landscape. A crucial scene that relates to this wider discourse of employment begins with a gentleman who is seen, on the floor, looking for the perfect box of eggs (see Figure 2.3). While this looks like nothing more than an eccentricity in the first instance, another customer entering the store sheds some light on this situation. This eccentricity is said to be the result of his career. She notes that this is something that she has seen elsewhere and that in every instance the people reduced to this are always high school guidance counsellors. The reason, according to this woman, is – as she puts it – 'If your job served as little purpose as theirs, wouldn't you lose it, too?' Randal seems to concur at this point, noting that his guidance counsellor was 'pretty worthless.' This tacit assent leads to the punchline of the scene; the woman leaves on the line 'See? It's important to have a job that makes a difference, boys. That's why I manually masturbate caged animals for artificial insemination.'

In response to this, a critic could focus on lines extending into the farming industry, agricultural practices, and *their* role in the American economy in the early 1990s, but to do so would, frankly, be to miss the point. This joke is a throwaway line, played purely for laughs: there were many different versions before they settled on the manual masturbation of caged animals. Before being cast as Randal, Jeff Anderson was initially in line

Figure 2.3 Another customer searches for 'the perfect box of eggs.'

to take this role, 'only at the time the character was killing chickens for the railroad' (Muir 2012). While always demonstrating caution when we speak of 'intent,' this excised line reveals something about how this scene is expected to play with the audience. In essence, it is a string of words approaching meaninglessness, a violent action linked to a corporate entity with only the opaquest of motives or justifications. The role of guidance counsellor may be so worthless, to borrow Randal's phrase, that it drives the people who fill that role crazy. However, even the people pushing the message of valuable work are engaged in work that has no real meaning or significance. The entire discourse – when pushed by anyone outside the youth group themselves – is, perhaps appropriately enough, a form of masturbation. When work offers no meaning, the obvious question is, how does one spend the time at work in a way that can generate some meaning or pleasure of its own? The next chapter will turn to how, to borrow a phrase from Stuart Hall and Tony Jefferson, strategies employed by youth subcultures 'solve, but in an imaginary way, problems which at the concrete material level remain unsolved' (Hall and Jefferson 1976: 47).

Note

1 *Clerks* (2011) [DVD] Directed by Kevin Smith. USA: Miramax.

3 'Who closed the store to play hockey?'
Work and leisure

Turning to the subject of leisure so soon after, and within the discussion of a film bound up with questions of, the issue of employment invokes ideas most associated with Thorstein Veblen, in *The Theory of the Leisure Class* (1899). It was in this book that Veblen theorised that the rise of a leisure class – one whose leisure was conspicuous, even flaunted – arises because over time labour becomes 'a mark of inferiority, and therefore comes to be accounted unworthy of man in his best estate. By virtue of this tradition labour is felt to be debasing, and this tradition has never died out' (Veblen 1994: 36). Veblen himself might be surprised to find later critics using his ideas to describe a Generation X slacker such as Randal in *Clerks* since he explicitly says in the book that 'an habitual neglect of work does not constitute a leisure class' (22). Nevertheless, the post-industrial world of the late twentieth century was a very different world from the industrial one that Veblen observed; that Randal's work has implications beyond those he anticipated is perhaps one of the smaller and more predictable differences between the two eras.

This chapter, then, will engage with Veblen (and other theorists, such as Michel de Certeau) to consider a period in which young Americans became disillusioned with their career prospects and consequently began to think about the other things they could be doing with the hours they spent at work. This is best demonstrated by invoking the economic concept of 'opportunity cost,' which Colin Drury defines as 'a cost that measures the opportunity that is lost or sacrificed when the choice of one course of action requires that an alternative course of action be given up' (Drury 2005: 36). Longer hours and greater commitments to a career are generally undertaken because of the belief that people will get more out of that effort, whether that is measured in material wealth or status. By the 1990s, however, young Americans had lost faith in the idea that material wealth would ever come to them in the way it had come to their forerunners in the Eisenhower era. At the same time, status was seen by several sections of Generation X as something that conveyed little meaning and – as an external source of validation rather than one born of an authentic self – would never bestow happiness.

In turn, some members of this generation would begin to think about life as experiences, rather than primarily in terms of acquisition. If one revisits Douglas Coupland's *Generation X* for a moment, one encounters two definitions that provide the reader with a useful window into this topic. The first is 'Poverty Jet Set,' which the novel describes as 'people given to chronic travelling at the expense of long-term job stability or a permanent residence' (Coupland 1991: 7). In itself, this offers a challenge to the world that Veblen sketched at the end of the nineteenth century. At that time, he observed that the accumulation of goods was in itself a key social signifier, serving to demarcate one's place within class and social hierarchies:

> in any community where goods are held in severalty it is necessary, in order to his own peace of mind, that an individual should possess as large a portion of goods as others with whom he is accustomed to class himself.
>
> (Veblen 1994: 31)

Abandoning the acquisitive strategies that played an essential role in marking one's place in American society, then, is a substantive break with previous practices, even if – as in Coupland's novel – the kind of experience that one undertakes starts to signify one's capital in what are sometimes comparable, if not precisely similar, ways to the ones observed by Veblen.

The second term is the 'anti-sabbatical,' which is a job taken only for a limited time. The novel tells us that 'the intention is usually to raise enough funds to partake in another, more personally meaningful activity such as watercolor sketching in Crete or designing computer knit sweaters in Hong Kong' (Coupland 1991: 40). What these definitions share is an inherent challenge to the assumptions of the purpose of labour – the idea of building and sustaining a home is particularly problematised here. Instead, these two notions prioritise the idea of *leisure* over the security that a long-term career and home ownership are supposed to offer. Cultural capital has come to mean more to this group than economic capital. With little opportunity to expand one's cultural capital in the post-industrial job market, leisure (and what one does with it) starts to assume more central importance in young people's lives.

Given Coupland's emphasis on leisure and his young characters' greater interest in the acquisition of lived experiences rather than material accumulation, it is imperative to examine the role of leisure in western societies at this time. Gerald Fain has outlined the importance of leisure for humans, when writing natural connectedness to those importances that have been humanity's foundation: beauty, goodness, truth, the sacred. Particular instances of beauty, goodness, truth, and sacredness focus, but do not exhaust, the transcendence that is proper to the important [...] This is not conceit. This is not another example of a new or young profession claiming importance [...] our sense of importance would be incomplete without an appreciation of leisure, as it would be incomplete without, for example, a full understanding of the place of art or religion in human experience.

(Fain 1991: 2)

This particular focus on transcendent importances necessarily brings one back to the subject of Romanticism, because the idea of transcendence has long been one of the central planks of Romantic thought. The idea of transcendence, experiences, or knowledge outside of the range of typical human perception is central to Romantic writing and philosophy, and several of the concepts that Fain invokes in the paragraph above, such as truth, sacredness, and beauty, have been fundamental to the work of Romantics as diverse as Kant and Keats. In the American tradition, the philosophy of transcendentalism had been one of the major movements of nineteenth-century Romanticism. The individualism that suffused the transcendentalist movement would go on to be a prominent figure of American Romanticism through the twentieth century. By the 1950s, the Beat movement was producing 'manifestoes of a neo-romantic counter-culture: manifestoes that were just as opposed to the official materialist culture of the United States as were Emerson's *Nature* and Thoreau's *Walden* in their time' (Alsen 1996: 35–6). The previous chapter noted the desire of the American man in earlier generations to retreat from society towards a wilder place of freedom, one more conducive to the individual spirit and often one free from the pressures of the mechanisms of capitalism. There is perhaps no more famous example of this in American letters than the transcendentalist Henry David Thoreau, whose writings about his time living around Walden Pond eventually became the book *Walden* (1854). If one follows this line of thinking, then, we find echoes of this Romantic individualism in *Clerks*. Social pressures corrupt the purity of the individual self, and it is through leisure – itself a form of retreat from the pressures of the working environment – that actual knowledge of the self becomes possible.

It is apparent to even the most casual or uninterested viewer that the two central characters in *Clerks* do not enjoy their role in the world of work. What is perhaps less apparent is that the two engage in a series of activities and strategies that turn their work life into something more akin to a leisure activity to render their existence in this sphere more bearable. These range from subtle tactics that initially seem like no more than slacking, such as in-depth philosophical conversations about matters that appear deceptively facile, to more blatant, directly insubordinate acts that have a clear crossover with leisure activities as they are more traditionally understood.

Slacking in the workplace as leisure

The first of these shown in the film is primarily motivated by the idea of 'slacking.' Unsurprisingly, given his contempt for the job that he holds, Dante's attitude to his work is one of near-total lack of commitment. Following the traumatic experiences of the early morning, he takes shelter behind the desk in the arms of Veronica. She is generally one of the driving forces to get Dante out of the store and to get him to try and achieve his potential. One of the ways that she uses her influence is to try and get him to go back to school as a way of escaping what she suggestively refers to as 'this pit.' Dante, however, finds more creative ways to escape work as his handling of the cash register demonstrates.

Dante gets around this particular responsibility of his job by leaving a plate of small notes and change on the counter with a sign asking people to leave their money and take the right change, with an exhortation to 'be honest.' The film does not show any of these customers in any detail, though we can hear coins being left, to which Dante calls up his thanks. When Veronica asks about the efficacy of this honour system, Dante suggests that the system works because 'Theoretically, people see money on the counter and nobody around, they think they're being watched.' Once again, any positive interpretations one may have had about his system are erased. Without his comment, one might see Dante as someone who believes in the inherent goodness of the members of his society and might see his stance as a refusal to inflict undue surveillance on people. Indeed, he might even come across as a transcendentalist, rather than exhibiting the supposed nihilism more commonly ascribed to his generation. Instead, this comment reveals that he is playing on their *expectation* of surveillance and that he can trust these people only because they would assume that no one could be that trusting. This pessimism is in keeping with the ironic and questioning tone not only of the film but of Generation X humour in general. Beyond the humour, however, it is clear that genuine thought has gone into *how* and why this would work. It relies on some actual philosophy concerning what it means to be a human living in society. There is a depth to this kind of tactic that the film's flippant dialogue can obscure.

Dante is also willing to engage in more active pursuits during his working hours. The film begins with his complaint that he cannot come in because he has a scheduled hockey game in the afternoon, and he only agrees on the proviso that he will be relieved *prior* to his leisure activity. After discovering that his boss will not be coming to relieve him, Dante questions whether they need to play their hockey game at the park – and after making an arrangement on the phone, suggestively asks Randal, 'You feeling limber?' Dante's decision to play a game like hockey in the store has the flavour of youthful rebellion. However, Michel de Certeau proposes another way to see this, through his theory that part of the appeal of such sports is that 'they exercise that function precisely because they are detached from those everyday combats which forbid one to "show his hand" and whose stakes, rules, and moves are too complex' (De Certeau 1988: 22). His boss has well and truly outmanoeuvred Dante, and though this game offers some measure of recompense, it also represents a movement to a form of leisure in which Dante has a far better understanding of the rules of the game. It is a retreat from work, then, not just in terms of slacking on the job, but from the kind of manipulation people are subjected to while at work. After Dante's question, the film transitions to a close-up of an arm wrapping the end of a hockey stick with tape, followed by a sequence of shots of various pieces of hockey equipment. The soundtrack at this point in the film is an abrasive, loud guitar-driven track by the independent rock band, The Jesus Lizard, anticipating the physicality that is about to come. After seeing them prepare, the game starts to take place, and this music begins again (see Figure 3.1).

This scene presents a curious interrelation of several different elements. The act itself, of closing the store to play hockey, represents a challenge to the paradigm by which one is paid to perform a role. It is made even more glaring as it takes place on the roof of the store. This placement offers a

Figure 3.1 Dante and Randal prepare for a game of hockey on the roof of the store.

complication of space, emphasising the disparity between the action and the characters' role still more than merely closing the store to play in the park or, as Randal suggests, the street, would have done. With Dante's solution, this leisure activity takes place both literally and figuratively *over* work activity. The coarse independent soundtrack, in turn, anticipates not only to the violence of the event but serves to frame this event within the discourses of independence mentioned in Chapter 1. This game is leisure not only for itself but leisure as an opting out of the work environment in favour of one where, as in de Certeau's comment above, the rules are far simpler. It is also a direct result of the actions of Dante's boss, and for both reasons, the leisure we observe cannot be easily separated from work; instead, it operates within a complex, mutually dependent relationship. Dante uses the fact that he told the boss he had a game and the boss still chose to go to Vermont to justify playing the game on the roof of the store. Implicit in this is a statement about the extent to which one's work can control and define them. In breaking store policy, Dante is refusing to allow his job to interfere with his plans. The manager (and, implicitly, his generation) can manipulate and control the younger employees and their time because they need to work within a capitalist system, but this only stops them doing what they want to do if they internalise those rules and follow them to the letter. Unsurprisingly, Dante gets no argument from Randal, the avatar of the slacker philosophy, who opines that 'insubordination rules.'

The game opens a site at work that is *not* work, one that prevents the grinding nature of employment from erasing Dante's individuality. However, this does not take place in an uncomplicated fashion: the film would be very different if Dante were successfully able to 'stick it to the man' by merely playing a game of hockey on the roof. Let us not forget that this is a film about a *nightmare* day at work, and the game itself cannot escape that. It is the store customers who, once again, act as the catalysts for Dante's misery. Most notably, one customer, who arrives and is unhappy that he cannot conveniently use the convenience store, begins to observe the game, and his conversation turns – in equally discontented fashion – to Dante's hockey abilities. The game is supposed to be a leisure activity for Dante, where he can relax and unwind through physical exertion. However, he is now scrutinised by the very people he moved to the roof to escape. This customer eventually figures in the game's *denouement*, as he goads Dante into letting him play with his critical commentary and then, with a stick in hand, smashes the ball as far as he is able. That this ends the game raises significant questions and links the game back to overarching narrative strands of the film. The most apparent leisure activity of the film lasts only twelve minutes. Dante laments the fact that they have only brought one ball with them, a foolish oversight that puts them into their current position. But Dante must also take his share of the blame, since it is his idea to play at the store, and crucially, to play on the roof, thus necessarily raising the chances of losing balls. Potentially, then, it is the inability to adequately plan and prepare for the game – by Dante as much as anyone – that, in the end, prevents the game from being a particularly useful retreat from work. Furthermore, if one recalls de Certeau again, Dante finishes the game stressed and complaining because a customer – someone who plays a part within the system of capitalist exchange he was looking to escape – has entered the game and has bested Dante by playing outside of what he understands as the rules of the game.

This scene is, as previously stated, Dante at his most rebellious. However, and perhaps predictably, Randal is still more committed to leisure in the workplace than Dante. He keeps to his own hours, arriving for work late and disappearing from the video store as and when it suits him. More significantly, his tactics for dealing with the customers are far more confrontational than Dante's. The latter literally hides from customers in the example above, while Randal sits in full view of the customers reading magazines, *visibly* slacking on the job. When challenged, he engages in games to amuse himself at the customers' expense. A notable example comes in one of the rare times he is seen at work in the video store rather than hanging out with Dante, in a scene where a customer cannot decide which film to watch. Consequently, she is attempting to solicit his opinion on the choices at hand (see Figure 3.2). This request seems an innocent enough action in the first instance. However, it does not take much thought to conclude that Randal's

Figure 3.2 A customer tries to trick Randal.

opinion of the movie has little bearing on whether she – someone of different age, gender, and social grouping – will enjoy it.

Nevertheless, this is not quite as ridiculous as her comment that the marketing material 'never tells you if it is any good.' This proposition both implies a singular quality of 'good' that can be objectively assessed, and that the marketing materials for a film would ever actively give you a reason *not* to rent a movie that it is their job to sell. With typical intolerance for customers asking questions that he considers stupid, Randal responds in non-committal fashion to the point that she attempts to trick him by holding up the same videos twice and getting different responses each time. From here, she insinuates his manager would not appreciate him paying scant attention to customers, to which he replies, 'I don't appreciate your ruse, ma'am.' Randal is consistently more verbally dextrous than the customers with whom he must deal, and he can use that deftness of expression to turn the situation to his advantage, turning his interactions with customers into a form of leisure. Randal upends the moral coordinates of the situation, and rather than being guilty of not doing his job well or paying attention to the customer, he is able to indict said customer for the lie told in trapping him. He goes further: when she defensively argues her case, he implies that she is sanctimonious, replying 'I hope it feels so good to be right. There is nothing more exhilarating than pointing out the shortcomings of others, is there?' Exasperated and insulted, the woman (credited only as 'indecisive video customer') becomes one of a long line of customers who swear at Randal and leave.

In addition to these verbal games, Randal is uninhibited in turning the store, generally, into a place of recreation with his friend. He acts like customers are not there, not only by ignoring them to read but by refusing to modify the tone and content of his conversations with Dante. One example is the scene in which Randal asks Dante about the 'jizz-moppers' at the 'nudie booths' and how much they earn. As a discussion of a work role, especially one that does not track to traditional notions of a career or long-term prospects, this conversation might well have had a place in the previous chapter on employment. Similarly, the fact that this conversation turns to what nudie booths are and what one can see in them might make it fit just as easily with the discussion of sexuality and masculinity that follows in Chapter 5. The most revealing part of this conversation, though, is that a customer walks up to the counter during this discussion and Randal continues as if the two clerks are alone. Eventually, and after a graphic recount of the booths themselves, his description of the role of the mopper finally causes the offended customer to speak up. 'The jizz-mopper's job is to clean up the booths afterward, because practically everybody shoots a load against the window, and I don't know if you know or not, but cum leaves streaks if you don't clean it right away.' The outraged customer replies that the use of such language in front of the public is cause for them both to be fired, with predictable responses from each of the two clerks: Dante attempts to pacify the customer, while Randal is unmoved. Instead, he doubles down, by showing the customer the centrefold of the pornographic magazine that he is reading: 'Well, you think that's offensive [...] then check this out. I think you can see her kidneys.' The customer runs away in horror.

These acts might look like nothing more than childishness or a petty refusal to leave adolescence behind – a kind of arrested development. But this kind of interaction and the games that the clerks – and Randal in particular – play with the customers are indicative of a more comprehensive strategy for coping with the demands of the workplace. These tactics become clear when considering an idea put forward by Michel de Certeau, who writes that

> Innumerable ways of playing and foiling the other's game (*jouer/ déjouer le jeu de l'autre*), that is, the space instituted by others, characterize the subtle, stubborn, resistant activity of groups which, since they lack their own space, have to get along in a network of already established forces and representations. People have to make do with what they have.
>
> (De Certeau 1988: 18)

This is what is evident in *Clerks*, a variety of strategies and mechanisms of resistance built into the established networks of the service sector. That they have the space to be as rebellious as they are – and to turn the store into a site of leisure – is nothing less than a sign that the owners of the stores care no more about this work than they do themselves. This is signified most clearly by the fact that Dante is here, unsupervised, while his manager disappears to Vermont. The only difference between Dante and his manager is that this member of the older generation is in the position to escape the store as and when they want. Therefore, these acts of resistance are necessary; customers in the film challenge the clerks by suggesting that the job is not particularly demanding and that they would enjoy having something requiring as little labour, but what they ignore is the dispiriting side of this work. Resistance is – in true Romantic fashion – a space for the individual to reassert that spirit in the face of stultifying corporatism.

Popular culture as leisure

This idea of 'making do' to form sites of resistance to the workplace can be seen in another instance, one that involves the mobilisation of popular culture. Here, though, the media saturation considered to be so typical of postmodern living and a defining characteristic in Generation X membership is turned to the advantage of the young, while also giving the film some of its most memorable dialogue. One of the most significant and meaningful leisure activities that Dante and Randal enjoy while working at the store is talking about *Star Wars*.

This choice is not without its significance. Given their age, the two protagonists would have been – like many in the target audience – children at the time the first film in the franchise became a smash hit and in their low teens when the trilogy concluded with *Return of the Jedi* (Marquand, 1983). They are dealing with texts that are, in some respects, formative for the members of their generation. However, their age is not the only reason that the choice of these films is significant. *Star Wars* is, like many other texts in the science fiction genre, an outpost of what is sometimes called 'geek culture.' Kunyosying and Soles suggest that 'Luke's development from the whiny, naive hayseed of *Star Wars* to the confident Jedi of *Return of the Jedi* constitutes one of the most influential geek narratives of the period' (Kunyosying and Soles 2012). And indeed, to champion things that are outside existing canons of 'good art' is an essential aspect of subcultural taste:

> Liking the same things differently, liking different things, less obviously marked out for admiration – these are some of the strategies for outflanking, overtaking and displacing which, by maintaining a permanent revolution in tastes, enable the dominated, less wealthy fractions, whose appropriations must, in the main, be exclusively symbolic, to secure exclusive possessions at every moment.
>
> (Bourdieu 1994: 282)

Liking *Star Wars*, then, is partly an enjoyment of childhood nostalgia, but it simultaneously operates as a kind of rebellion in the realm of taste, which in this film additionally combines with the characters' resistance to and rebellion against their work environment. Until fairly recently the central texts of geek culture were often portrayed as childish or feminising, and the embrace of them issues a challenge to the mainstream idea of what it means to be an adult man (this volume will return to this idea in more detail in Chapter 5). At the same time, the insistence that these are good movies worthy of time and effort operates as a challenge to the accepted canons of film. The characters' conversations by far exceed a simplistic analysis and delve into philosophical issues at the heart of the franchise's narrative, an understanding of which could only stem from the investment of that time and effort.

In this, they are reflecting a trend in fandom that Henry Jenkins identifies in his book, *Textual Poachers: Television Fans and Participatory Culture* (1992). Here, Jenkins theorises that fans, far from being mindless, passive consumers, are engaged and active in the production of meaning above and beyond those often explicitly relayed by the texts' producers. One of the most significant developments in this respect is that the fans in his study complicate the boundary between high and low culture. He notes that 'reading practices (close scrutiny, elaborate exegesis, repeated and prolonged rereading, etc.) acceptable in works of "serious merit" seem perversely misapplied to the more "disposable" texts of mass culture' (Jenkins 1992: 17) Nevertheless, the fans that he observes – be they fans of *Star Trek*, *Beauty and the Beast*, or any of the other shows that Jenkins examines, employ these strategies in their viewing of, and subsequent participation with, their favourite segments of popular culture.

Clerks is far from the first film in which characters have dramatically reproduced this activity on-screen. In fact, Smith would have seen an example in the film that inspired him to become a director in the first place, Richard Linklater's *Slacker*. Near the beginning of the film, an unnamed character gets into a taxi. He speaks at the driver in something of a monologue for the rest of the scene, his speech peppered with references to cultural artefacts and practices such as Leo Tolstoy, Frank Zappa, the 1971 film *The Omega Man* (Sagal), and channel hopping. The text given the most significance in that scene, though, is *The Wizard of Oz* (Fleming, 1939), invoked in order to explain the content of a book (which was, in fact, the product of a dream):

> the premise for this whole book [...] was that every thought you have creates its own reality, you know? It's like every choice or decision you make, the thing you choose not to do, fractions off and becomes its own reality, you know [...] and just goes on from there forever. I mean, it's like [...] uh, you know, in *The Wizard of Oz*, when Dorothy meets the Scarecrow and they do that little dance at that crossroads [...] and they think about going all those directions [...] then they end up going in that one direction. I mean, all those other directions, just because they thought about it, became separate realities. They just went on from there and lived the rest of their life. I mean, entirely different movies, but we'll never see it, because, you know, we're kind of trapped in this one reality restriction type of thing.
>
> (*Slacker*, 1990)

In this example, the unnamed character uses a well-known item of popular culture from the golden age of Hollywood to explain a difficult philosophical concept. It is probably safe to assume that this kind of enquiry was far and away beyond the goals and ambitions of the crew at Metro-Goldwyn-Mayer in 1939 even if it might have preoccupied L. Frank Baum, the author of the books upon which the film was based. It is also clear that the character has an intimate knowledge of the film, born of repeated viewing, since he does not refer to one of the more famous lines, set pieces, or songs from the movie but to a moment that demonstrates tremendous familiarity with the details of the plot.

In *Clerks*, though, Smith changes things in one fundamental respect: *Star Wars* is not used as a way of describing abstract conceptual materials but instead as a leisure activity, the discussion of which becomes another in a list of tactics for dealing with the mundanity of working as a clerk. Its power in this arena arises because it is treated as a matter of some importance. Rather than reducing it to a cogent analogy, the *Star Wars* trilogy (as it still was in 1994) is itself the subject of serious discussion. An easy way into understanding how they discuss these films is to look at their responses to the question first posed by Randal as to preference for *The Empire Strikes Back* (Kershner, 1980) or *Return of the Jedi*. Dante chooses perennial fan-favourite *Empire*, and as his explanation suggests

> Empire had the better ending: Luke gets his hand cut off and finds out Vader's his father; Han gets frozen and taken away by Boba Fett. It ends on such a down note. And that's life – a series of down endings. All *Jedi* had was a bunch of Muppets.

Dante – as pessimistic here as the rest of the film would lead us to expect – reproduces a highly Romantic viewpoint to validate his preference. His belief that the more sombre ending reflects life more closely, and therefore demonstrates more truth, is fully compatible with longstanding Romantic notions about art and its function. This is not even particularly complicated by the fact that this truth can be found in the impossible realm of the Space Opera since Romanticism has a long history of incorporating notions outside the boundaries of strict realism in favour of greater, poetic truth.

Randal breaks with the orthodox fan position – refusing to conform even to the expectations of his own subculture – and endorses *Return of the Jedi*. Rather than making such an explicitly Romantic defence of the film, Randal instead starts to read into the *Star Wars* universe things that the text itself does not gesture towards in any conspicuous way. Randal's examination of the film revolves around the idea that, unlike in *A New Hope*, the Empire had not finished building the second Death Star at the time of the Rebel attack in the third film. His reading rests on the idea that this is a more morally questionable act, that attacking something that is still being built is necessarily more suspect than targeting a strictly military site. Randal argues that 'All those innocent contractors hired to do a job were killed – casualties of a war they had nothing to do with.' On seeing that Dante is confused by his reasoning, he expands on his idea:

> All right, look – you're a roofer, and some juicy government contract comes your way; you got the wife and kids, and the two-story in suburbia – this is a government contract, which means all sorts of benefits. All of a sudden, these left-wing militants blast you with lasers and wipe out everyone within a three-mile radius. You didn't ask for that. You have no personal politics. You're just trying to scrape out a living.

The world of the Space Opera is usually governed not by the rules of our own world but by its own generic conventions, mostly bracketed from the everyday by the dominant readings of the text. Randal, though, has rewatched *Return of the Jedi* repeatedly. That familiarity with the text means that he sees details in the plot which, in turn, open narrative possibilities. The combination of textual details with observations taken from the world around him – incongruous as they may initially seem with the world of the Space Opera – leads him down some intriguing philosophical avenues. Discussion of these possibilities operates as a kind of leisure, not least because talking about one's favourite film is more pleasurable than dealing with the realities of menial work. The scene ends with Randal somewhat repudiated, though, as an actual roofer gives a real-world example of turning down a job that subsequently got someone killed before weighing in that any contractor on the Death Star would have known the risk, and it would have been their own fault. He concludes, pointing to his heart, 'a roofer listens to this, not his wallet.' Randal and Dante's engagement with *Star Wars* in this way has an intriguing ending. The owners of the franchise have not always been the most receptive to fan-led interpretations and productions. Jenkins writes that 'Lucasfilm initially sought to control *Star Wars* fan publications, seeing them as rivals to their officially sponsored and corporately run fan organization' (Jenkins 1992: 30). However, George Lucas actually addressed the discussion on the director's commentary on the DVD of *Star Wars: Episode II – Attack of the Clones* (Lucas, 2002), though seemingly misremembering it as an exchange between the more famous Jay and Silent Bob.[1] A film that is – in part at least – a fan production found itself influencing, in a small way, an instalment in the franchise that inspired this dialogue in the first place.

Along with the more obvious games and the simple act of talking about preferred films with friends, in *Clerks*, leisure can also be found in the most unlikely of places. In fact, the wake that the two attend becomes something of a leisure event, especially for Randal, who sees it as 'the social event of the year.' Randal does not have the connection with the deceased that Dante has (though we might question how *moved* Dante really is, anyway) and treats this as a gathering, a chance to do something other than work. This framing is the crux because, although we only see them travelling to rather than at the wake, it is another moment in which the store is closed and work stops so that the two can prioritise another, more preferable activity. They drive to the wake while listening to the alt-country group Golden Smog, then signed to the independent label Rykodisc. The wake itself takes place off-screen. We see the two protagonists walking up to the funeral home, with sombre music in the background. The screen then cuts to a card that says, 'five minutes' later, and we hear a thud and a woman's scream. When the pictures return, we see Dante and Randal racing to their car (see Figure 3.3). The funereal sounds of the previous scene have been displaced by 'Leaders and Followers' by Bad Religion – a band signed to major label Atlantic at a time close to the film's production but who had become important players in American punk through the 1980s while releasing several albums on the independent label Epitaph. The scene ends with the two protagonists driving away as angry relatives chase them and hurl things at the departing car. On their arrival back at the store, it is revealed from their conversation that their rapid getaway had been prompted by Randal knocking over the casket.

This entire scene is in keeping with the tone of the film. The sense of humour borders on surreal and gestures towards the socially inappropriate, though again, the worst excesses of slapstick and 'bad taste' all take place off-screen. This choice is no doubt in part due to pressures of budget, but

Figure 3.3 Dante and Randal fleeing Julie Dwyer's wake.

it also makes for a compelling narrative device. It allows the film to flirt with the absurdities of these images without the pressures of attempting to dramatise them. The reports that we get of such events are, in themselves, revealing. Randal is attending this event as a social gathering, and given that he is the most forthright voice of a slacker mentality in the film, it cannot be a coincidence that it is the slacker who has caused an uproar that has them needing to make a quick getaway because he was 'leaning' on something. A problem has been caused for the two clerks since one was slacking in an inappropriate social situation.

As this chapter has demonstrated, there is a difference in the way that Dante and Randal interact with the customers. Indeed, Dante tries to push that still further, claiming that there is a fundamental difference between the acts that each commit and the reasons underlying them that render his resistances unavoidable and certainly more acceptable than those undertaken by Randal. Dante tries to justify his actions – taking time off to attend the wake and play the hockey game – as different from Randal's efforts to avoid work, because he says these are obligations happening at a particular time. Closing the store for those things cannot be avoided without missing them. It is a difference, essentially, between work interfering with things that can *only* happen at a specific time and doing whatever you want, whenever you feel like it. In turn, this assertion leads to a philosophical discussion between the two about their role in the store and how much freedom it gives them, as Dante says that Randal cannot do whatever he feels. Working in the store gives them specific responsibilities. Randal replies, 'so your argument is that title dictates behaviour?' He turns this by comparing their situation to a death squad soldier in Bosnia. Dante scoffs, saying the comparison is unfair because he is not being asked to kill children. This brings only a retort of 'not yet,' another dark, comedic interjection that casts moral aspersions on the management of the store and the structure that governs their lives. It is at this point that Randal spits water in the face of the customer reading the tabloid headlines (as mentioned in Chapter 2). He does this partly because the customer is annoying him but more explicitly because he claims it proves his point about it being he who determines his behaviour, rather than his job. Following this demonstration, Dante agrees to give Randal the keys to his car, and though he does it with a gesture of resignation one wonders if there is more than a little truth in it when Randal says, 'you know I'm your hero.'

Perhaps the most explicit reasoning for the importance of leisure in the workplace comes – again, unsurprisingly – from Randal. Before he finally snaps at Dante, he needs to endure a rant about how he does not take his job seriously (and how, in turn, that causes problems for Dante). During this rant, every defence that Dante offers relates to leisure. He does not spend as much time as he should in the video store, because he prefers to spend time talking to Dante in the convenience store. He leaves to rent a video from the other store because he wants the two of them to watch the film he rents *together*. In the final reckoning, then, the job they do can be a cause of misery for them, but Randal has transcended that by concentrating on what he can get out of it, which is friendship. There is a bond here for Randal, one that is far more satisfying than his job, and ultimately that means it is of far greater importance.

In this film, then, youth employment is presented as both uninspiring and manipulative. Rather than simply give way to that, though, the protagonists turn the situation to their advantage wherever possible. Using the strategies implied by de Certeau's idea of making do and Jenkins idea of being 'textual poachers,' Dante and Randal are able to push back against the strictures of their job. These leisure activities they engage in as a result may not have the obvious political resonances of the counterculture of the late 1960s, but regardless of their apparent frivolousness these responses are of tremendous importance for the individual subject.

Note

1 *Star Wars Episode II: Attack of the Clones* (2002). [DVD] Directed by George Lucas. USA: Lucasfilm.

4 'I still get free Gatorade, right?'

Clerks, youth, and consumption

The setting is much more than a mere backdrop to a story; rather, it is a vital element that informs the spectator's interpretation of all other characters and interactions. Experience of all texts is shaped by the world in which the events take place, as the locations in which plots play out create meaning and carry inference. For example, *12 Angry Men* (Lumet, 1957) works in large part because of the cultural connotations of the jury room, while if *Office Space* (Judge, 1999) were set in an amusement park it would have been a very different film. Consequently, *Clerks* – set almost entirely in two stores – is a film inextricably bound up with ideas of consumption, one that deals with what and how we consume, as well as the experience of working as a small part of the service industry that is dedicated to consumer culture.

However, consumption is of more fundamental importance here than the necessary relation between action and location. Dick Hebdige wrote that the kind subculture to which *Clerks* appeals is 'concerned first and foremost with consumption [...] it operates through commodities' (Hebdige 1979: 94). Also, as the previous chapters have endeavoured to show, *Clerks* is not only a film that struck a chord with a certain subgroup of young people in the 1990s but is a product of a distinct youth subculture. For critics like Thomas Doherty, consumption is tied to the very idea of a youth culture in the first place. Youth cultures are not concepts that are a historical given; instead, they come into play at particular historical moments. For instance, the idea of teenagers as a distinct social demographic emerges in the US and similar countries in the period following the Second World War. This historical moment relates to all manner of cultural trends, including the relative affluence of the 1950s that put more money into the pockets of a young group for the first time in US history. As Doherty puts it, they were 'set apart from previous generations of American people in numbers, affluence, and self-consciousness. There were more of them; they had more money; and they were more aware of themselves as teenagers' (Doherty 2010: 34).

This identification led, in turn, to marketing to youth as a distinct group set apart from the rest of the nation, as chasing the dollars of the young provided a fillip to the American consumer-based economy. Lawrence Grossberg suggests that 'by 1957, the juvenile market was worth over $30 billion a year. This was the first generation of children isolated by business (and especially by advertising and marketing agencies) and an identifiable market' (Grossberg 1992: 173). Of course, such changes were not without their critics, with popular authors and cultural commentators alike pointing to the harming effects of the marketisation of youth. For instance, Rob Latham writes that Ron Goulart's *The Assault on Childhood* (1969) 'was designed to warn parents that their children were gradually being lured into a commercial relation with faceless outsiders whose motives deserved close scrutiny' (Latham 2002: 43). Later, Neil Postman would write *The Disappearance of Childhood* (1982), a text that 'attributes a determining significance to technologies' and displayed a desire 'to turn back the clock' to a time before television (Buckingham 2013: 26–7). It appears that youth cultures of this period prompted anxiety in as much as they seemed to be markers of more considerable social change.

Equally, the development of youth consumer culture in the 1950s had significant corollaries in cinema and music. Before the mid-1950s, Hollywood studios made no real sustained effort to make films specifically for youth audiences. That changed during the middle years of the 1950s when a series of films 'challenged the conventional understanding that movies were to be viewed by the family [...] by being marketed specifically to teenagers' (Slocum 2005: 2). Following the huge success of *Rock Around the Clock* (Sears, 1956), a low-budget film designed to exploit the chart success and impact of Bill Haley and His Comets' titular song, Hollywood would never look back. From there, 'the popularity in its wake of an imitative cycle cast from the same mold, first testified to the present power and future ascendency of the teenage moviegoer' (Doherty 2010: 55). Rock 'n roll had changed music, driven primarily by money in the pockets of the young. The same conventions and culture saw Hollywood cinema create an entire genre. These films would often feature icons of the era such as Bill Haley or Elvis Presley, though other actors in this period would also become megastars due to their association with rock n' roll iconography. For instance, James Dean became a symbol for the young generation, despite not playing in films that were specifically designed to exploit youth culture, while Marlon Brando, who was approaching 30 when he appeared in the *Wild One* (Benedek, 1953), was also strongly associated with the youth culture of the time on account of his leather attire and overall anti-establishment attitude. The connection, then, between youth cultures and consumption is one of tremendous importance. Never before had there been a period in history when the young had been understood as a distinct demographic with marked differences between what they and other groups consumed.

Since the 1950s, successive generations of young people in the US experienced youth cultures that were intricately linked to consumerism even if in certain instances that relationship was threatened (as was the case during the late 1960s and early 1970s when counterculture became a significant force in US society). However, while businesses and advertisers had identified the young as a potential band of consumers for several decades, the generation who were the audience for *Clerks* necessarily had a different relationship to consumer culture because they were disproportionately likely to work in the industries that serviced that culture. Unlike their predecessors, however, the chances of moving into other fields were getting poorer as employment patterns shifted and the US, like many other nations, grappled with the fallout of the post-industrial age. The politics of the era reinforced these changes, as the ethos of the consumer spread beyond its existing boundaries to reform – or, depending on one's perspective, infect – other aspects of life. As Don Slater suggests, 'Exemplified in neo-liberalism – specifically in Reaganomics and Thatcherism – consumer choice became the obligatory pattern for all social relations and the template for civic dynamism and freedom' (Slater 1998: 10).

Artistic responses did not always endorse these changes. A sharp image near the beginning of Douglas Coupland's *Generation X* is of dogs who have made their way into the dumpsters outside a cosmetic surgery centre, and, consequently, 'their snouts are accessorized with [...] yuppie liposuction fat' (Coupland 1991: 4). We are dealing here with extreme wealth, one accumulated by a competing subculture of broadly young upwardly mobile professionals (yuppies) that made their presence felt in American society and popular culture in the 1980s just before (and alongside) the moment Gen Xers started to enter the word of work. As a subculture, yuppies can not only afford processes like liposuction but tend to consume so much that the provision of services like liposuction is commercially viable. This is not simply cosmetic surgery but the medical removal of the consequences of excess. Beyond this, there is a clear parallel between the consumption of the dogs, who mindlessly consume fat pulled from the bodies of Californian yuppies, and the same processes that swelled the waistlines of those same yuppies in the first place. Though this is a particularly gruesome metaphor for consumption beyond what is needed (or even healthy), the concept extends far beyond food to all manner of consumer goods. One of the principal characters, called Claire, works on the Chanel counter at I. Magnin and says

> I develop this weird feeling when I watch these endless waves of gray hair gobbling up the jewels and perfumes at work. I feel like I'm

watching this enormous dinner table surrounded by hundreds of greedy little children who are so spoiled, that they can't even wait for food to be prepared.

(Coupland 1991: 11)

The narrator tries to mitigate some of Claire's criticisms, but even so, it is hard to escape the judgement here. These customers come from a segment of society that voraciously consumes luxury goods with the same gluttony that might be exhibited by small children.

In the condemnation of older, wealthier members of the community as greedy and spoiled, we might be inclined to think so far, so familiar to subcultural polemics. Consumption, however, relates to more than just hamburgers and diamonds, and *Generation X* effectively indicts its protagonists in a world of thoughtless consumption equal to that of the yuppies and Baby Boomers condemned in its early pages. Embittered as they are by their exclusion from the economic opportunities available to their parents, Gen Xers retreat from the world. Though the greed and gluttony they see elsewhere in their society repel them, their retreat is itself a form of consumption; instead, they voraciously consume information from the media that is all around them. Though the grand narratives of their civilisation seem to crumble around their ears, smaller bite-sized chunks of narrative are always available through their televisions. Programmes originally aired either in their youth or in the 1950s heyday of television that coincided with a period of economic optimism seem to have displaced engagement with the wider world. This media saturation is no real replacement, though, and Coupland is clear that their alienation is in part because this is a scant substitute for genuine optimism about one's situation in life.

> This nagging awareness that commodity culture offers only a pale sustenance – and that irony is a necessary but insufficient response to the situation – coexists, in the psyches of Coupland's characters, with an abiding resentful perception of how this commercial system mercilessly preys upon them.
>
> (Latham 2002: 193)

Consumption and customers

Such, then, is the representation of consumer culture in *Generation X*, a crucially significant novel for youth culture in the early 1990s. By contrast, *Clerks* is a text that is less explicit as a statement regarding a specific cultural moment but one that in other respects deals even more closely with the topic of consumption. To appreciate why this film might be important in understanding consumption for this group at this time, one might also consider the biographical component in play. Kevin Smith's first film has always intrigued people, in part, because it was shot in the very same store in which he had worked. As such, it offers us something of the perspective of someone employed in one of these jobs and a flavour of how he viewed the experience. Ultimately, though, his working in a small, suburban convenience store that has a video store next door is remarkably serendipitous. Dante and Randal work in stores that, between them, provide the small essentials of everyday life (rather than dealing in larger transactions) and act as one of the lower rungs in the media distribution network. There are perhaps no two better places to offer comment on the situation that a young person found themselves in at this American cultural moment. However, if one is interested in the employment of the two central characters because they are seen at work, one is at least as interested in the primary purpose of those spaces and the representation of their *function*. As stores, these spaces are necessarily tied to capitalism and to the service industry that had grown into an ever more prominent section of the American economy in the previous decade.

As *Clerks* presents it, consumption is central to the society in which we live. One of the first scenes of consumption in the film demonstrates the critical understanding of consumer culture in microcosm. We see Dante, manipulated into going into work when he would be sleeping, greedily glugging coffee to revive himself enough to perform his job. But the only reason that he holds the job he hates in the first place is to buy consumer goods – presumably including the coffee that he drinks. In this one moment, as throwaway as it might seem, we see Dante locked into a cycle of work and consumption. However, if this consumption is an integral part of our society, then in *Clerks* our society is inherently dishonest, for consumption and consumer culture are no neutral series of exchanges conducted in good faith. Instead, this is a dog-eat-dog world, one in which dishonesty and subterfuge are essential tools that are deployed in both subtle and crude forms. One joke that emphasises this is that to acquire the newspapers sold in the store, Dante effectively steals them from an automated booth outside. Previous chapters have already discussed several instances in the film where Dante seems to want to escape from the sharp practices that buffalo the individual subject in the everyday world. However, this one image shows us that Dante is himself no dewy-eyed innocent. He knows the same tricks and is quite as willing to engage in them as anyone else, no matter how overwhelmed he can sometimes become. The main characters are also just as prone to resort to consumption as a panacea, as seen in Randal's response to Dante's miserably asking, 'why do I have this life?' His sole response is to offer him some potato chips.

A telling instance of the same gamesmanship in the film occurs in the scene in which they are going to play hockey. Seeing that the usual rules have broken down, one of Dante and Randal's fellow players asks if he can have a free bottle of Gatorade. Dante initially tells him that he cannot, pointing out that, if he does it, everyone is going to want one, and asking (quite reasonably) who is going to pay for all those bottles of Gatorade. The retort that Dante is selectively enforcing only some aspects of store policy (given that he is preparing to play hockey on the roof during regular opening hours) carries the day. The game itself only lasts twelve minutes, yet the same player asks if he can still have his freebie. A few minutes later the audience learn that the various players have between them consumed the store's entire stock of Gatorade. Dante is manipulated by his friends so they can bypass the usual rules of exchange and consume without the usual costs.

This association of consumption and manipulation also extends to one of the most famous comic set pieces in the film. Immediately following the slide 'Vilification,' a man (Scott Schiaffo) who has ordered a drink asks if he can drink it there but starts to ask customers as they order cigarettes to consider what they are actually buying. The first customer is asked when he started smoking and how old he is before this gentleman drops something down on the counter and pronounces 'that's your lung. By this time, your lung looks like this.' He follows that by handing him a 'trach ring' used in medical procedures in the throat, before adding, 'This one came out of a sixty-year-old man.' Dante nervously attempts to intervene, but in the first instance the customer speaks with more authority and continues his theme, eventually handing the young shopper a pack of 'Chewlies Gum,' which he gets him to take instead. The scene ends with Dante asking him not to bother the customers, but the next person who wants to buy cigarettes asks what is on the desk, so we infer that despite Dante's efforts these events are about to repeat themselves. When the film returns to this thread (having introduced the audience to the characters Jay and Silent Bob) a crowd has gathered around the anti-smoking advocate, and he speaks with the righteousness of a preacher (see Figure 4.1). This troublesome customer turns the crowd of would-be smokers by initially concurring with their statement that we all must die someday before turning it around, saying that does not mean we have to pay for it. The comedy of the scene comes, however, when he turns his attention towards Dante, drawing a false equivalency between his role as a clerk in a convenience store that happens to sell cigarettes and the genocide perpetrated by the Nazis in the 1930s and 1940s: 'Friends, let me tell you about another bunch of hate mongers that were just following orders: they were called Nazis, and they practically wiped a nation of people from the Earth [...] just like cigarettes are doing now!'

62   '*I still get free Gatorade, right?*'

Figure 4.1 A 'customer' turns a crowd against Dante.

The nature of the setting creates an opposition between Dante behind the counter and those on the other side. While usually this would potentially designate power or authority to the person behind the counter, in this case the advantage is clearly with the greater number of people. This is partly because the ludicrousness of the comparison catches Dante off-guard and partly because the scene itself problematises the idea of any authority in this position. His presumed authority is, in some sense, contingent on consumption and on those people who would consume items from the store respecting his position. Here, that is undone by a single firebrand who can convince the mob to hurl back the cigarettes at Dante while they shout, 'cancer merchant.' In so many ways, cigarettes are the ultimate consumer product – something without clear use value (since they kill the consumer rather than hold benefit) and once you are addicted to them, they must be purchased on a repeated basis every day.

The end of this scene is perhaps the most pertinent. At one level, knowing all we do about the dangers of smoking, we might have some sympathy towards the cause this character is espousing, even as we laugh at the ridiculousness of the argument he puts forward. The film undercuts this possibility, however, when in his final moments in the store Dante's girlfriend Veronica reveals that he is a representative of Chewlie's Gum. This is the very brand that he has mentioned several times during his angry tirades, and it becomes apparent he has been drumming up anti-smoking feeling in order to drive the consumption of that brand of gum. This scene, then, displays scepticism about those conveying what might be interpreted as positive social messages, because even here we cannot escape the influence of capitalism and consumption. The humour here rests on the presumption of ideological purity – that the value of an action is dependent on it being wholly altruistic, without gain to the self. It is easy to come up with a line of reasoning that could argue the motives of the salesman are irrelevant if his actions lead to people spending less and living longer. However, the reasoning of the film – and, as we have seen elsewhere, much of the philosophical underpinning of this youth subculture more generally – sees his cause as suspect because he lacks disinterestedness. In a sense, this reflects the capitalist tendency to market rebellious anti-consumerist lifestyles and symbols back to youth cultures, and *Clerks* joins in with the grunge response to acknowledge and laugh at the way that this happens. We might, then, see in this the tragedy of the Generation X mindset – the inability of the individual Romantic subject to escape the effects of capitalism – played for laughs.

The salesman is just one of many problem customers that Dante and Randal have across the course of the film. The real problem of consumer culture seems to be the customers, both in their entitled attitude towards the young people who must serve them and in their peculiar habits. The motto of American business might be that the customer is always right, but *Clerks* mocks that idea by showing the American consumer at their most insulting or bizarre. One of these nightmare customers is central to the plot of the film. An older man turns up asking to use the toilet, though this quickly turns into a series of exchanges in which he manipulates Dante in giving him free things. He asks to use the toilet playing off his medical needs, citing age-related incontinence. The situation develops as he moves into an area with financial consequences, convincing Dante that his haemorrhoids will not cope with the 'rough' toilet paper in the bathroom. Dante agrees, after some cajoling, to allow him to take a roll of the more expensive paper that the store sells. free of charge. The third question leaves behind the question of medical need entirely as he asks for something to read – in the process, this older man is coaxing his entertainment out of the clerk without paying for it. We progress quickly from a newspaper to pornography, and since by this point, Dante is no longer putting up any resistance, the 'customer' starts to make requests for *specific* magazines. Consumption here has left behind any medical need, moved through comfort, through basic entertainment and is now in the realm of specialist entertainment, with the 'customer' taking advantage of the clerk in order to subvert the model of the store. Through manipulation, he gets the services that the store offers provided to him for free. This exploitation of Dante ultimately leads to the old man dying during a bout of frenzied masturbation in the bathroom, with consequences that will be explored more fully in the next chapter.

Venerable men with a penchant for masturbating in staff bathrooms are, again, far from the only nightmare customers that Dante and Randal encounter. Several unpleasant exchanges were documented in the first chapter, but there are several more that have specific implications for the idea of consumption in America. However, if these first examples strike us particularly exceptional, then others are, at their core, staggeringly banal. This too is apt, since

> Consumer culture is largely mundane, yet that mundanity is where we live and breathe, and increasingly so as we sense that the public sphere of life has become a consumable spectacle that is ever more remote as a sphere of direct participation. 'Consumer culture' is therefore a story of struggles for the soul of everyday life, of battles to control the texture of the quotidian.
>
> (Slater 1998: 4)

The convenience store in which Dante works is, quite literally, at a nexus of where people live; contemporary society would not operate without the distribution of food and other essential goods that such stores provide. In *Clerks*, though, the battles we see play out for the soul of everyday life are reduced to the level of absurdity as customers invest mundane, everyday objects with a significance beyond easy comprehension. This significance then necessarily impacts on the lives of the protagonists, whose job it is to serve these consumers. One example that has already been briefly touched on is the odd man surrounded by open cartons of eggs as he looks for the perfect dozen. Dante tells Randal that the man has been doing this for twenty minutes and that 'he yelled at me' when Dante suggested he took eggs from different cartons to make up a perfect dozen that way. The scene leads into the revelation, as mentioned earlier, that this man has been driven mad by his role as a high school guidance counsellor, but, intriguingly, this insanity manifests itself in his attitude towards consumer goods, in this case, foodstuffs. The eggs are perfectly useful in and of themselves, regardless of whatever odd characteristics the man looks for, but this arbitrary distinction becomes oddly valid in the world of American consumerism. We laugh at the man for the absurdity of searching for the perfect egg. However, consumer culture is predicated on the notion of those kinds of distinctions between items with similar use value in the first instance. Moreover, the presumption of the consumer is that no matter how ridiculous or personal their demands, it is the role of the retailer – and the underappreciated staff who work in that industry – to cater to them.

During the film, Dante and Randal discuss at some length the types of customer that annoy them. This critique is instigated, unsurprisingly, by Randal, while Dante needs to be goaded into saying what he really thinks. Eventually, he owns that there are certain traits – or groups of customers – that bother him, and he begins by citing 'the milkmaids,' whom he describes as 'The women that go through every gallon of milk looking for a later date. As if somewhere – beyond all the other gallons – is a container of milk that won't go bad for like a decade' (see Figure 4.2). At first glance, this seems similar to the behaviour of the man looking for the perfect box of eggs: people acting eccentrically in and around mundane household products. Here, though, there is a clear difference. In the case of the individual looking for the perfect dozen eggs, what he searches for is an abstraction – as we are never privy to what he means by perfect eggs, there is very little meaning in the quest other than that which he, alone, gives it. The 'milkmaids' on the other hand are examining something accessible to us all – nothing as conjectural as the angles of an egg but sell-by dates on the bottles, written as clear as day in standard English. And yet there is still something ridiculous about what they do, emphasised by Dante's comment that they are looking for milk with a ludicrously long lifespan. As a perishable product, bottles of milk available in the store will be reasonably close to one another in terms of their shelf life. One must ask what drives the milkmaids to spend time searching for something as unlikely as milk that defies the progress of time.

One of the underlying points about consumer culture is that 'Material Goods are not only used to do things, but they also have a meaning, and act as meaningful markers of social relations' (Lury 1996: 12). With that

Figure 4.2 The milkmaid, played by Smith's mother, Grace.

in mind, suddenly, several possibilities open up. In this case, the search for a never-spoiling bottle of milk has less to do with the milk itself and more with questions of how one relates to other participants in the system of exchange. The selection of the 'right' bottle of milk out of a field of options with insufficiently long lifespans would act as an important marker designating that this is a woman who cannot be conned by the providers of such household goods. At the same time, such a signifier would also demonstrate that she was a more discerning customer than her peers, one more skilled at some aspects of homemaking. Nevertheless, of course, the need to demonstrate one's thriftiness, one's Baby Boomer values through the pursuit of a product that does not exist is laughable.

Randal continues this conversation by noting the kinds of customer he hates. As has been noted in earlier chapters, Randal differs from Dante in some fundamental ways – their attitude to customers is far from the least significant difference. The principal idea of their role is that they are there to serve the customers of the store: perhaps an obvious point, given that they work in the service industry. However, Randal, in particular, seems to have flipped that notion on its head. As already discussed, he comes in late or not at all, depending on his whims. At the beginning of the vignette titled 'Syntax,' Randal explains how he ripped up the membership card of someone who was refusing to pay late fees because Randal had arrived two hours late for work the previous day, thus hindering his ability to pay. When Dante calls this a 'shocking abuse of power,' Randal retorts that he is 'a firm believer in the philosophy of a ruling class. Especially since I rule.'

All kinds of things are visible in this exchange. On the one hand, there is the mixture of philosophical discourse familiar to treatises on the proper nature of government with the language of Dante and Randal's subculture. On the other, we have this sense of the carnivalesque, with Randal using the scant authority his position provides to run the store essentially for his own convenience and amusement. One such example is Randal's restocking of the store's pornographic section while a young mother and her child stand in front of him. After being asked for the fictional movie *Happy Scrappy – The Hero Pup*, Randal says to the distributor:

> I need one each of the following tapes: *Whispers in the Wind, To Each His Own, Put it Where It Doesn't Belong, My Pipes Need Cleaning, All Tit-Fucking Volume Eight, I Need Your Cock, Ass-Worshipping Rim-Jobbers, My Cunt and Eight Shafts, Cum Clean, Cum-Gargling Naked Sluts, Cum Buns Three, Cumming in a Sock, Cum on Eileen, Huge Black Cocks with Pearly White Cum, Girls Who Crave Cock, Girls Who Crave Cunt, Men Alone Two – The K.Y. Connection, Pink Pussy*

'I still get free Gatorade, right?' 67

Lips, and *All Holes Filled with Hard Cock*. Oh, and […] what was the name of that movie?

Initially, this seems little more than a laundry list of filth and is partially reminiscent of a game of one-upmanship in which the film entertains by naming increasingly explicit titles. However, the potentially subversive nature of Randal's action is brought home by the anecdote that the actor, Jeff Anderson, refused to read this line in front of the woman and child, and so the scene was shot to make it look like they were in the same room at the same time instead.[1] Taken in this light, what might initially seem to be simply puerile can instead be seen as something of a challenge to the accepted conventions of suburban, middle-class society, even if we must always recognise that the pornographic section of the video store also *serves* that same section of society.

Given Randal's attitudes generally, one should not be surprised to hear that the customers Randal says he could do without are 'the people in the video store […] All of them.' The montage that follows suggests that Randal might well have a point. The first customer asks, 'What would you get for a six-year-old boy who chronically wets his bed?' This question either makes no sense or – if we accept the basis of the question as legitimate – is far beyond the training (and the remuneration) afforded to people working these jobs on the lowest rung of the service industry ladder. There is a danger in taking what could be a throwaway comic line seriously, but one cannot expect to get free paediatric psychology advice in a video store. While the remaining customers – in this particular montage, at least – do not expect medical advice, there is still a clear tendency to make unreasonable demands of the people who serve them. One asks if there are any new movies while standing in front of a massive sign advertising new releases. Another asks, 'Do you have that one with the guy who was in that movie that was out last year?' Both examples are excessive demands because they play into the negatives of American consumer culture. In each case, the customer does nothing to help solve their own problem, instead laying even the most elementary work – such as bothering to read a sign or remembering any of the details associated with the film they are looking for – at the door of the store clerk.

Consumption and cultural capital

Randal's dislike for the customers of the store is not prompted simply by their exploitation of people who work in these roles. It is also tinged by notions relating to cultural capital – or, to put this another way, his attitude is influenced by the kind of media he consumes. In this, despite his representing a youth group, his attitude is nothing new. Veblen, writing in the nineteenth century, observed that

> The criteria of a past performance of leisure therefore took the form of 'immaterial' goods. Such immaterial evidences of past leisure are quasi-scholarly or quasi-artistic accomplishments and a knowledge of processes and incidents which do not conduce directly to the furtherance of human life.
>
> (Veblen 1994: 45)

In other words, the way that one demonstrates one's membership in the leisure classes is by demonstrating a refinement of tastes that would be considered impossible in those who had to spend their time working. The idea of such a leisure class – or at least of Randal's belonging to it – feels out of place. Nevertheless, the idea still has some validity if one replaces the purely class-based understanding of this refinement with a commitment to gaining more familiarity with the material or – perhaps more troublingly – the idea of an *innate* ability to perceive more deeply than others. These ideas are what we can identify in Randal's attitude. He complains that the people in the video store 'never rent quality flicks; they always pick the most intellectually devoid movie on the rack.' This quickly turns into a joke at the expense of the 1990 action film, *Navy SEALS*, directed by Lewis Teague. Randal laments that 'It's like in order to join, they have to have an IQ less than their shoe size.' Randal's thinking might initially seem to make quite the conceptual leap here. To understand this conflation of taste and intellect, we should remember Jenkins' observation that 'Because one's taste is so interwoven with all other aspects of social and cultural experience, aesthetic distaste brings with it the full force of moral excommunication and social rejection. "Bad Taste" is not simply undesirable; it is unacceptable' (Jenkins 1992: 16). Dante responds, mentioning stupid questions he gets asked, as the film cuts to another short montage in which one customer is surprised the coffee they ordered has to be taken hot, followed by another asking the price of an item while standing in front of a sign detailing its cost.

But one thing is clear; the way Randal mocks the video store's customers for the type of media they consume links back explicitly to the kinds of discourse around subcultures and independent cinema that have been discussed elsewhere in this volume. The media that the people who patronise the video store (and, by implication, the convenience store) consume give an impression of them that can be understood better when one considers the work of Don Slater:

Yet we also have an image prevalent in both everyday life and social theory of the consumer as a dupe or dope. This consumer – the mass, conformist consumer – is defined precisely by its failure to live up to this standard of 'maturity,' of reason and autonomy. Firstly, the consumer as dupe is a slave to desires rather than a rational calculator of them, is defined not by its formal rationality but by its substantive desires, whims, impulses. Its desires are not autonomous but determined by others, by the needs of family, by social pressure, by fashion and trends, by advertising, marketing and the media. Indeed, the everyday consumer is not seen as the rational calculator of self-defined desires but rather as the *object* of rational calculation by other forces, the target of a marketing drive or advertising campaign.

(Slater 1998: 55)

The humour at work here – laughing at someone who wants to watch *Navy SEALS* – creates a binary opposition between the knowledgeable consumer and the mass conformist consumer, one reminiscent of the dichotomy between American independent cinema and Hollywood. This binary romanticises the idea of independent filmmaking and implies that there is something less discerning about the consumer of Hollywood movies. At the very least, one would determine from this scene that the people who enter the store have poor taste, but in the way that this is structured – with poor taste conjoined to poor attitudes and poor questions – the idea of intellect comes more into play. These are people duped by American consumer culture, those unable to act as the rational calculator of what they need and who instead respond impulsively. They are at the mercy of Hollywood and its contrived plots and narratives just as much as they are hoodwinked by advertising and other psychological tricks of consumer culture more generally. Given the attitudes of both American independent cinema and alternative youth subcultures towards 'the mainstream' and a perceived conformism, this vein of humour is well judged for the likely audience of *Clerks* – it is not implausible that the people who bought alternative rock albums and watched independent cinema also thought that the audiences who turned out for *Navy SEALS* and similar militarist blockbusters were deficient in taste, intellect, or both.

Nevertheless, *Clerks* does not entirely fit the model of American independent cinema that we have seen elsewhere in that it has a much stronger 'youth' dimension and less emphasis on 'high art.' Consequently, though there are some attitudes towards popular culture that one might see as elitist, in truth, this is also a world rich in the imagery of that same popular culture. Rather than dealing with a simple hierarchy then, we are dealing with the judgements made between different items that belong to the same realm. The distinction is not between high and low art but between forms of popular culture that are or are not valued by this particular youth subculture – something that one knows instinctively if one is a member of this particular group, almost like some kind of shibboleth. As Thornton says:

> Tastes are fought over precisely because people define themselves and others through what they like and dislike. Taste in music, for youth in particular, is often seen as the key to one's distinct sense of self. Youth, therefore, often embrace 'unpopular cultures' because they distinguish them in ways that the widely liked cannot.
>
> (Thornton 1996: 164)

Being on the right side of the equation with a group affords one what Thornton refers to as *subcultural capital*. In the case of *Clerks*, central to this seems to be films that the two (and, by extension, those of the same age sharing similar inclinations) would have watched as children or teenagers. An example of pop culture that one might almost miss without paying close attention is Randal pushing a potato chip around a jar of salsa, partially submerged, so it resembles a fin, while he hums the theme from *Jaws* and quotes lines from the movie. We have already seen, too, how Randal quotes lines from *Indiana Jones and the Temple of Doom* and the extensive way that the two discuss the *Star Wars* franchise. There is also something quite revealing in the fact that when they are discussing the respective merits of the *Star Wars* franchise, Dante praises the darker of the two sequels (as of 1994). His argument is that 'Empire had the better ending.' This darkness could be seen to reflect not only an understanding that this is somehow more adult, more honest or serious, but that it also fits in with an aesthetic tendency common to both grunge and alternative rock (as opposed to pop music). One might even extend this to the often-dark humour of *Clerks* itself. It cannot be a coincidence, either, that while the two engage in talking politics through the medium of *Star Wars* and in taking certain jobs, the camera focuses on Jay, who is stealing by surreptitiously eating things straight from the packaging. Once again, the system of exchange on which consumer culture is based is one of deception, of exploitation, and of taking shortcuts to get what you can for the least outlay.

The attitude towards pop culture and work come together in the way that Randal demonstrates his own ability to discern a good film from a bad one. Randal asks Dante to lend him his car because he wants to rent a movie. The apparent irony here, of course, is that Randal works in the video store next door and does not need to go anywhere to rent a movie. In fact, given his attitude towards work, he could get one free of charge, whether this was an authorised perk of his job or not. He is, therefore, choosing to inconvenience Dante to go and get a film from another video store. His reasoning is related to the consumption of popular culture. He has nothing but contempt for the place where he works, including not only the clientele but the kind of films that they stock. Randal wants to travel to what he sees as a better store, to get what he considers a good movie. When we see Randal in the store, we see him walking through a bright environment with well-stocked shelves and appropriate music that speaks to the world in which he now finds himself, and he falls to his knees in delight at what is available to him (see Figure 4.3).

Finally, though, the film does call into question many of these attitudes. Randal's final rant challenges some of the assumptions made about consumption in the rest of the movie. If elsewhere the film implies that the people who come into the convenience store or the video store are inferior, it is Randal – the embodiment of that attitude – who undercuts it by asking why they work there if they are better than the patrons.

> We like to make ourselves seem so much better than the people that come in here, just looking to pick up a paper or – God forbid – cigarettes. We look down on them, as if we're so advanced. Well, if we're so fucking advanced, then what are we doing working here?

How one reads this turn at the film's conclusion might say more about the politics of the individual viewer. Is this the film at its bravest, giving an unpalatable truth back to the slacker generation about their own

Figure 4.3 Randal falls to his knees in joy at the 'good video store.'

shortcomings and complicity with the problems that face the world? Or is it instead the film abandoning a countercultural position and re-inscribing a dominant ideology in its *denouement*? In truth, either reading is entirely plausible, though it is also worth pointing out that this kind of self-awareness is not utterly alien to this generation. As one woman of this generation told a journalist in 1994, "'We're spoilt, rotten brats [...] Slap Us!'" (Freedland 1994).

Note

1 Revealed by Kevin Smith on the director's commentary of *Clerks*.

5 'Any balls down there?'

Clerks, slacker masculinity and sexuality

So far, this volume has considered how *Clerks* arises from a network of discourses of independence, and the film's opposition to dominant social paradigms. Unsurprisingly, this applies not only in the explicitly political realm of youth employment and consumer culture but also in the more *implicitly* political realm of masculinity. Indeed, masculinity was a topic very much enmeshed in political discourses in the US during the 1980s. In a 1983 piece for the *Washington Post*, Ellen Goodman wrote that Ronald Reagan held such a strong position in the American imagination that he could afford to be more emotional than most of his peers. She opined that, unlike Reagan, 'one man [Democratic Senator for Maine Ed Muskie] lost his bid for the presidency because of half-a-dozen tears mixed with the New Hampshire snow' (Goodman 1983). This focus on gender inevitably went beyond President Reagan and permeated several different ideas of the presidency more generally. Around the same time, John Mihalic wrote that Jimmy Carter failed as the Executive because he had lost his masculine credentials once he entered the White House, finally concluding that 'in a sense, we've already had a woman President: Jimmy Carter' (Mihalic 1984: 30).

Though rarely made this explicit, it is clear looking back that masculinity was an apparent political concern in the late 1970s and 1980s. Much of this relates to shifting social dynamics, as western societies altered in line with the pressures placed on them by a new, post-industrial labour order. Emergent economies that were expanding elsewhere inspired the decline of the traditional industrial and manufacturing sectors in the US. Taken together, this prompted a downturn in the types of work by which men had traditionally defined themselves, as well as increasing casualisation in remaining jobs (Elliot 1996: 75). This deterioration was felt in the pocket of the average American – and particularly in the pocket of the average American man:

> young white families earned 20 per cent less [...] in 1986 than did comparable families in 1979, and their home ownership prospects

plummeted. Real earnings for young men between the ages of twenty and twenty-four had dropped by 26 per cent between 1973 and 1986, while the military route to upward mobility that many of their fathers travelled constricted.

(Stacey 1996: 32)

The decline in men's wages combined with changes in attitudes towards gender roles through the 1960s and 1970s, and this confluence of economic and social factors led to men's role as the head of the household being less secure than it had been a generation previously. Susan Faludi tells us that, as a result,

> in the 1980s male nerves rebelled [...] as a 'decline in American manhood' became the obsession of male clergy, writers, politicians and scholars all along the political spectrum, from the right-wing Reverend Jerry Falwell to the leftist poet and lecturer Robert Bly.
>
> (Faludi 2010: 85)

These social shifts did not occur without resistance from some on the American right. A renewed clamour for politics organised around what might be (with a deal of caution) thought of as 'Family Values' rose to attempt to arrest this decline in the privileged position of American manhood. Conservative critics blamed the diminished position of men, and particularly of fathers, for any number of American social ills, including crime, violence, and declining educational standards. This social transformation had become a central issue from an era before the Reagan presidency through to the time that *Clerks* was made and beyond:

> Backlash sentiment against the dramatic family transformations of the past four decades has played an increasingly pivotal role in national politics in the United States since the 1970s, when the divorce rate peaked, and a national White House Conference on The Family that was planned during the Carter Administration fractured into three, deeply polarised, regional conferences on families convened during the first year of the Reagan Administration.
>
> (Stacey 1996: 3)

The family values agenda, then, proved particularly resilient, running through the 1980s and outlasting the Republicans' hold on the White House. Citizens who hoped that the country would pivot away from a socially conservative agenda after Bill Clinton won back the White House for the Democrats in 1993 were soon disappointed. As Stacey suggests,

'Startlingly soon after his election, Clinton too jumped on the family-values trolley. Republicans and Democrats alike now compete to promote their politics in the name of the family – meaning one particular kind of family' (Stacey 1996: 4). Family values – and the images of masculinity that this kind of politics implied – had achieved a level of political orthodoxy by 1994, bridging the party divide.

The social changes of the past decades had been reflected in – and perhaps even exceeded by –Hollywood's representation of gender. A content analysis of Hollywood films produced across the twentieth century seems to show that 'by the 1940s [...] many more women had begun to work outside the home, as well. In response to this turmoil in American life, Hollywood's female leads become much more interested in romance and family life' (Powers et al. 1996: 154). This suggests that Hollywood's reaction to shifts in gender roles and experiences in the 1940s and 1950s appears to be an attempt to cling to conservative notions and to reassert a traditional order, even if only symbolically. However, as the twentieth century progressed, questions arose as to how much that impulse dissipated, with Powers, et al. arguing that Hollywood representation changed at a much faster rate than mainstream American society. They write that 'many, if not all, of the earlier kinds of representation of women characters were modified, or even reversed outright, albeit in complex, interdependent ways' (Powers et al. 1996: 159). This argument implies that critical work suggesting the presence of a still-reactionary representation in Hollywood gender relations by the 1980s is incorrect.

Nevertheless, one cannot help but notice that the complex interdependencies that Powers et al. mention offer a great deal of cover for reactionary impulses. The authors understand Hollywood liberalism in the 1980s not within a context that approaches liberalism critically or in relation to other film industries and whether they represent culture in more or less liberal ways. Instead, they compare Hollywood's liberalism to other US institutions and elite groups (the military, the business sector), which have been traditionally dominated by strong conservativism (Powers, et al. 1996: 52). Not surprisingly, such an approach telegraphs Hollywood as much more liberal than perhaps was the case if it was compared to other film industries and institutions around the world, and at the same time understand liberalism and its representation in simplified terms. Whatever the final reading of the politics of such Hollywood texts – which might in the final reckoning be ambiguous, of course – and whether we believe that their cultural representations were in line with society or ahead of it, what is clear from Powers et al.'s position is that at some level the cinematic representation of women has changed as the nature of American work and family life has changed.

This shift in female representation may have been remarkable on its own terms, but for the purposes of this chapter, developments in the onscreen portrayal of *masculinity* are more intriguing. Famously, Susan Jeffords (1994) has written of Hollywood masculinity during the Reagan years in terms of 'Hard Bodies,' with its most clear manifestation being the hypermasculinity of heroes in the action movies that achieved incredible popularity across the course of the decade. Indeed, the first film that Jeffords examined in detail in her book, *Hard Bodies*, was the Rambo franchise, starring Sylvester Stallone as Vietnam veteran John Rambo. Jeffords argues that

> because the films focus on Rambo's physical prowess, and because Stallone himself did extensive body-building for the part, the films can be used to illustrate how the hard-body imagery evolved during the eight years that Ronald Reagan was in office.
>
> (Jeffords 1994: 28)

Stallone was not alone, of course, and her work also notes that the 1980s saw 'the molding of a former Mr. Universe into the biggest box-office draw of the decade,' referring to the tremendous popularity of Arnold Schwarzenegger (24). Clearly, then, there is a trend in 1980s Hollywood towards images of hypermasculinity, which connote perceived values such as toughness and physical fitness. These qualities then manifest themselves in larger-than-life muscle-bound heroes, something that was reflected elsewhere in the massive success of the World Wrestling Federation (primarily driven by the crossover appeal of the physically massive Hulk Hogan) and the popularity of TV's Mr. T.

However, by the early 1990s the trend for 'hard bodies' seemed to be coming to an end. By this point, and despite some examples as *Terminator 2* (Cameron, 1991) and *True Lies* (Cameron, 1994) in which stars like Arnold Schwarzenegger continued to flex their muscles, the big action stars were more likely to be playing comic roles that subverted their 1980s images, such as Schwarzenegger in *Kindergarten Cop* (Reitman, 1990), Sylvester Stallone in *Stop! Or My Mom Will Shoot* (Spottiswoode, 1992), and Hulk Hogan in *Mr. Nanny* (Gottlieb, 1993). Indeed, by 1994, the year of *Clerk's* release, the premier action hero of the 1980s, Arnold Schwarzenegger, would be seen giving birth in Ivan Reitman's comedy *Junior*. At the same time, American independent cinema and other cultural expressions representing subcultural groups that often placed themselves in direct opposition to dominant tropes provided numerous of examples of artists and texts that dealt with questions of masculinity in direct opposition to the 'hard body mainstream' of 1980s Hollywood. For instance, it is hard to find a more explicit rejection of this ideal than in comedian Bill Hicks – a cult figure who never cultivated an especially broad or mainstream audience – who, in a show recorded at the Funny Bone in Pittsburgh in 1991, said 'Hulk Hogan – another reason I PRAY FOR NUCLEAR HOLOCAUST WITHIN ONE MINUTE!' (Hicks 2009: 54). Similarly, the leading icon of the grunge movement, Kurt Cobain, did not reproduce the masculinity of action movies and the posturing of the big hair glam metal era of the late 1980s. In an era where size seemed to matter Cobain was decidedly on the small side (even before his well-documented heroin addiction) and far from physically imposing. To borrow a phrase from David Greven then, 'in terms of popular culture, the Bush 41 era was anything but status quo,' at least insofar as it concerns the question of masculinity (Greven 2009: 4).

In American independent cinema, the trend was similar, and one can see how key films from the sector found recognition outside the US for going against the Hollywood grain. Taking the Cannes Film Festival awards as a barometer, one can see how 'Best Actor' awards were given to actors and performances of a vastly different nature to those from Stallone and Schwarzenegger. Specifically, the American actors who won in the 1980s were William Hurt (playing a gay man imprisoned for sex with a minor in *Kiss of the Spider Woman* [Babenko, 1985]); Forest Whitaker (as the Jazz musician Charlie Parker in 1988's *Bird* [Eastwood – released by Hollywood major, Warner Bros.]); and James Spader (for his role as Graham Dalton in *sex, lies, and videotape* [1989], which did so much to change the landscape of independent cinema in the United States). These portrayals look inward far more than in the action movies of Hollywood, and, rather than dealing with hypermasculine figures, they instead focus on loners, drifters, artists, and criminals – men on the fringes of society or those who undermine normative values. The point is not to say that these characters are held up as alternative heroes but rather to suggest that independent film is interested in masculinities of a decidedly different stripe. These trends would continue to the point that Timothy Shary writes that 'challenges to perceived norms about sexuality and sexual preference, social identities and expectations, power and strength [...] have been especially manifest in feature films since the 1990s' (Shary 2012: 1).

Masculinity in *Clerks*

This latter kind of masculinity, then, is closer to the type that one encounters in *Clerks*. Where Smith's films operate around a pair of young men (as is the case not only in his debut but also in his two next features *Mallrats* [1996] and *Chasing Amy* [1997]) none conforms to a type of hegemonic masculinity. Typically, these men are aimless, indecisive, or have pursuits that tend more towards the arts or particular geek or alternative subcultures. As Carter Michael Soles writes,

> Smith's films depict the real tensions and dangers Generation X male slackers face as they attempt to negotiate the culturally enforced gap that separates male homosociality (intense friendship, male bonding) from explicit male-male homoerotic desire and homosexuality in contemporary U.S. culture.
>
> (Soles 2008: 6–7)

Soles' argument relies strongly on a queer thread that he claims runs through *Clerks*. Whether or not one agrees with this idea, *Clerks* is still a film that offers a presentation of young men attempting to negotiate a culture in which they are far from dominant figures. This culture seems to expect more from them than they can or are willing to give, and it is one in which their discourse is intensely bound up with sex and sexuality in intriguingly suggestive ways.

A key sequence in *Clerks* that engages directly with ideas of masculinity as a dramatic conflict, of sorts, between a 'hard body' and an embodiment of an alternate, subcultural masculinity takes place during the 'Paradigm' chapter. Dante is harassed at work by a customer who says he heard Dante strain when he hands him a bottle of milk, arguing that he needs to spend more time in the gym. There is a clear contrast drawn between the two. Dante is scruffy, dressed in the 'grunge uniform' of layered clothes and sporting a beard; the physically fit customer has fuller shoulders, wears a pristine white sweatshirt, and is clean-shaven. At this moment, two distinct versions of masculinity have come into contact. As we know, Dante represents an alternative subcultural masculinity. At the same time, this other figure stands like a living embodiment of the kind of normative masculinity espoused in Hollywood cinema through the 1980s. He tells Dante that he is a trainer (appropriately enough, given the value that hegemonic masculinity places on physical fitness), stressing that Dante does not get enough exercise, that he has 'no tone.'

As the scene progresses, a woman walks into the store, and the customer begins to solicit her opinion, asking her to comment on his body and whether he is in shape. He invites her to touch his arm, and after being complimented tells Dante to roll up his shirt, as the process of commenting on his body shifts into an open invitation to get other people to touch him. As the dialogue continues, it turns out that this is Rick Derris, who reveals that he used to sleep with Caitlin while Dante was going out with her, a revelation that places Rick Derris and his version of masculinity in a superior position, since he was effectively cuckolding Dante. It is not clear that the film necessarily seeks to endorse this so much as it is playing on a fear of alternative masculinities for a comic effect. Rick leaves just after Dante has been issued with the $500 fine for Randal's selling cigarettes to a child and shoulder bumps him out of the way. It is telling, too, that the girl he has been talking with is impressed with Rick, and when he asks if she lives somewhere says 'sure, how about the beach,' suggesting that she wants more than just a ride home. Dante's day gets worse through the whole exchange as he is humiliated by (and in front of) an embodiment of a competing version of masculinity.

Of course, the subcultural masculinity that Dante embodies is not simply the negation of the 'hard bodies' ideal; one must delve deeper to understand how this type of masculinity operates. Aaron Taylor writes of Adam Sandler films that 'Sandler's physiognomy and comic performativity evoke an anxious masculinity that is not merely juvenile, but instead is positively prepubescent. His frequent helplessness, compulsive vulgarities, jejune naïveté, regressive hostility, and romantic ineptitudes are indicative of a seemingly devolutionary masculinity taken to histrionic extremes' (Taylor 2012: 24). The main actors in *Clerks* have a less extravagantly physical style, but in more subtle ways we can identify the same impulses in much of their interactions. For example, the first few scenes of the film do a lot to establish frames of masculinity in relation to Dante and his perceived helplessness. The first time spectators encounter him it is as a character forced to work against his will – or, to put this another way, as a narrative agent whom things happen *to*, the passive victim of events rather than the active force who changes them – a characteristic that not only distinguishes him from the typical Hollywood protagonist that drives the narrative through their actions but which also has gendered implications that Simone de Beauvoir traces back at least as far as Aristotle (de Beauvoir 1997: 39–40). Dante complains about the turn of events but, aside from whining, does not offer any real resistance, a trait which will be repeated throughout the film. His next significant encounter is in the scene with the representative of Chewlie's Gum. Once again, Dante is unable to deal with the situation by himself. This time he is saved by the interference of Veronica. This moment in the film offers us a contrast between the two. Dante is passive, but Veronica is active from the start. Barring a brief shot in which she walks through the door, our first real sight of her is in a position of power, having leapt up to a freezer cabinet where she uses a fire extinguisher to subdue the mob (See Figure 5.1). Soles argues that her 'arrival and actions thereafter are formally structured to emulate a superhero comic book action sequence' (Soles 2008: 72).

However, given the dominance in the previous decade of the action genre, I would argue that there is an intriguing suggestion of the action hero about Veronica, or at the very least of that figure viewed through a comedic

Figure 5.1 Veronica, wielding a fire extinguisher, rescues Dante.

lens. Rather than being asked to laugh at Veronica, though, we should note that she deals with the situation with the use of a weapon, albeit a fire extinguisher rather than the semiautomatic weaponry familiar to the Hollywood hard-bodied heroes. She also takes control of the situation immediately, speaks in the kind of laconic register familiar to those heroes, and both saves Dante and exposes the identity of the 'villain' of the piece. The absurd nature of her pointing the nozzle of an everyday item as if it were the muzzle of an M60 never really reflects on her. Instead, it serves to heighten the absurdity of the situation in which Dante finds himself. While this raises other questions about the relationship between the film and gender – the ongoing centricity of the *male* character even while others are on screen is no doubt significant – it means Veronica can send up the action hero without the bizarre nature of the situation rebounding on her. In this, it has parallels with a near-contemporary Bond movie: 'in *Goldeneye* it is M who most convincingly performs masculinity, and she does so partly by exposing the sham of Bond's own performance' (Halberstam 2018: 4). There are few other commonalities between *Clerks* and *Goldeneye* (1995) or between the performances of Marilyn Ghigliotti and Judi Dench, but both upstage the masculinity of their film's male protagonists in ways that parody or disclose cinematic conventions.

The presentation of Veronica is crucial because her character is central to the film's framing of gender – and the relationship *between* the genders – early in the film. Once Veronica has vanquished Dante's tormentors, the two characters sit behind the counter. They are positioned so that Dante is almost cradled by Veronica; he sits in front of her, with his head laying back against her chest. There is an intimacy here, but the way that Veronica consoles Dante after his morning from hell borders on the maternal. Any traces of a parental relationship in their presentation stand in stark contrast with their conversation, which reflects a common interest of both young people, and American independent cinema more generally, in its frankness regarding sex. The two talk about the differences that the respective genders encounter as lovers, effectively establishing an opposition between their two roles. This opposition is perhaps still more intriguing given the fact that while Dante espouses attitudes that essentially downplay the woman's role, he lies in her lap painting her nails – hardly a behaviour that conjures associations of the alpha male (see Figure 5.2).

During this exchange, the two joke about having sex behind the counter. When Veronica tells him that she was kidding, Dante tells her that she cannot get enough of him – a moment of confidence and machismo that might seem jarring but instead creates quite a complex depiction of masculinity within Dante, who can move almost seamlessly between more dominant and alternative versions of masculinity. Veronica observes that this is, in some ways, a typically male point of view, remarking that 'You show some bedroom proficiency, and you think you're gods. What about what we do for you?' By contrast, Dante implies that things are much easier for women because their role is mostly passive. Veronica is unimpressed with his description of the woman's role – and presumably, her role – in their sex life and responds with incredulity to his comment: 'A girl makes a guy cum, it's standard. A guy makes a girl cum; it's talent.' All she can say in reply

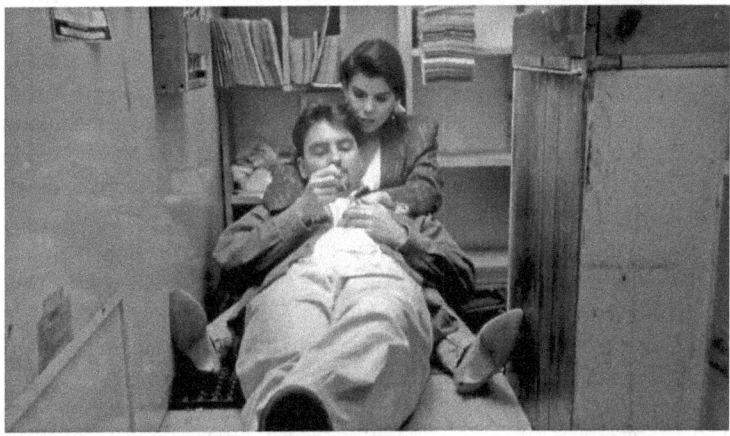

Figure 5.2 Veronica cradles Dante behind the counter.

is, 'And I actually date you?' – a sentiment that many in the audience might sympathise with by the end of the film.

Given this beginning and the nature of their conversation, it is unsurprising that sex is at the heart of the fight that sees Veronica storm off from the store and leads Dante's day from bad to worse. His fortunes change when a character called Willam (but with the nickname 'Snowball') enters the narrative. What follows that revelation is a description of the sexual practice that inspires this nickname: Veronica explains to Dante that 'After he gets a blow job, he likes to have the cum spit back into his mouth while kissing. It's called snowballing.' This dialogue is just one example of conversation around non-standard sexual activity throughout the film. Leaving aside the implications for masculinity that snowballing presents (if one stays focused on the relationship with Dante and Veronica the significance of this scene is that it is the cause of an argument), a few moments earlier, Veronica had listed the three men she had sex with, only to reveal that though he was not on her list, the Snowball nickname came about in part because she, herself, had 'snowballed' Willam.

Dante's response borders on the hysterical when he discovers that though Veronica has only had sex with three other men, her sexual history is more varied than that low number implies. Though Dante is quite relaxed about his own sexual history, he seems to rather like the fact that Veronica has only had sex with three men. The revelation that her additional sexual experience might significantly outstrip his own changes the equation. Dante begins yelling and the camera cuts away to show us that he has woken up the cat that has been sleeping in the store since the morning. A revealing moment occurs when Veronica challenges him that she did not react the same way upon learning of Dante's twelve sexual partners. Dante replies 'This is different. This is important. How many?!' Clearly, then, the number of women he has slept with is a matter of no real concern, but he nevertheless considers it his right to know about the sexual history of his girlfriend, and for him, it is a matter of some significance. While Veronica calculates the number of men on whom she has performed oral sex, a woman comes to the counter and buys something from Dante without saying a word, indicating that all of this is happening in plain sight. As if this were not enough, the public display becomes more apparent with Dante's exasperated comment to another customer, 'my girlfriend sucked 37 dicks.' Some decades later we might wonder if this constitutes a kind of public shaming of Veronica, but as this is a comedy, the scene is primarily played for laughs, perhaps never more so than in the customer's shocked response, 'in a row?!'

The two characters' different attitude to oral sex is suggestive. Veronica thinks less of oral sex than of penetrative sex as she does not list the men on whom she has performed fellatio among her lovers. Dante, on the other hand, tends in the opposite direction and frames it as if this is somehow *worse*: 'Well [...] why did you have to suck their dicks? Why didn't you just sleep with them, like any decent person?!' Soles attempts to draw out the significance of this opposition:

> Here Dante constructs normative, missionary style sexual intercourse ('sleep[ing] with them') as being 'decent' and thereby implies that Veronica's willingness to give blowjobs to her dates is indecent or deviant in some way. And indeed, the fact that Veronica has had oral sex with thirty-six guys implies that she is more sexually open than Dante, and her predilection for giving fellatio – an oral form of sexuality conventionally viewed as less developmentally mature than missionary style sex – queers her to an extent. Most importantly, and despite Veronica's reassurances, Dante sees this indecent/queer behavior of Veronica's as being a threat to his own position: 'Every time I kiss you I'm going to taste thirty-six other guys.'
>
> (Soles 2008: 80–1)

Whether or not one agrees with whether Veronica is 'queered' by the number of times she performs oral sex, one can still make some reliable inferences for masculinity as a result of this exchange. The construction of missionary sex as 'decent' implies a certain conservatism in Dante. There is something comic in this conservative reaction because of the contrast between this stance and the transgressive attitude that he had tried to cultivate earlier in the conversation with his suggestion that he sleeps with people with paraplegia because 'They put up the least amount of struggle.' It is also clear that Dante's response to the 'threat' to his masculinity is the misogynist suggestion that Veronica has somehow been marked – tainted, even – by her supposed promiscuity. She is uncowed by his attitude, however – unsurprisingly, given that she has been presented as more modern, more 'together,' and more in control of the situation than Dante. This sense of self-reliance extends into other areas. In a later scene, we learn she once changed his tire for him, to which Dante defensively replies 'Hey, I jacked up the car, all she did was loosen the nuts and put the tyre on.'

Eventually, the two repair the rift between them when Veronica brings Dante a lasagne for his lunch. One might be inclined to see this as a somewhat reactionary gesture in which the man is unreasonable and the woman still must make it up to him, and with food at that. However, an alternative reading is that this is another instance in which Veronica is *active*, bringing about change in the world and improving her situation. Conversely, Dante is *passive*, with the change in their relationship something that happens *to* him. Invoking another negative stereotype, one might think he is in the familiar role of 'wife-at-home' who sulks until the husband buys flowers to apologise for some perceived slight.

Veronica is not the only woman that Dante interacts with at length. Instead, they form two-thirds of a love triangle with Caitlin Bree. For much of the film, Caitlin is off-screen, talked *about* by the male protagonists rather than seen. She is framed in these conversations in numerous ways, from 'the one that got away' to 'the one that broke his heart,' depending mainly on Dante's feelings towards her, and towards Veronica, at the time. The first significant conversation about Caitlin revolves around Dante's belief that the two are on the verge of getting back together, a vision that falls apart when Randal shows him an announcement in the paper that says she is getting married. Later, Caitlin reveals she rushed back to address the misunderstanding with Dante because she knew on hearing of the engagement he would be an emotional wreck. When he denies this unconvincingly, she says that she 'loves a macho façade, it is such a turn-on.' This exchange offers us two key insights into the relationship. Firstly, Caitlin understands that Dante is far from self-sufficient and that news of his ex-girlfriend getting engaged would devastate him even though he was in another relationship himself. One might initially think that this displays a certain arrogance until we realise that she is entirely correct. Secondly, Caitlin's implication that his macho façade is an unattractive trait undercuts the idea that women want an alpha male, someone who can act tough. One cannot infer that these characteristics are unattractive in and of themselves because Dante would only be *performing* that kind of masculinity, but what one can surmise is that this kind of posturing is less attractive to the modern woman than simply being true to oneself. A gender scholar might cite Judith Butler to argue that all gender is ultimately a performance. However, despite the merits of any such reading, it is worth remembering that such views have little sympathy with a narrative (and cultural moment) as invested as it is with ideas of authenticity.

Once Caitlin appears, it becomes clear that Dante is attracted to strong women: while denying that she is going to be married, Caitlin states that she does not want to get married now, instead preferring graduate school and a focus on her career. If both Caitlin and Veronica are strong, modern women, this is not the only thing that they have in common, and Dante also relates to certain aspects of their personality with consistency. We have already seen that Veronica's sexuality threatens Dante, and later in the film when Caitlin (by her own admission) throws herself at Dante, he suddenly pivots away from the flirtation that largely constituted his conversation to this point. Rather than either going along with what had been his own suggestion a few seconds earlier or even merely continuing to flirt, Dante instead begins to lament the fact that Caitlin is sexually promiscuous. His insecurity in this matter leads him to lash out at Caitlin in much the same way that he felt the need to fight with Veronica; for him, she is marked by her sexual history. Dante makes the snide remark that her sexually charged suggestion of spending time together is something that he has heard is 'a rather popular date.' He also asks pointedly about her fiancée, a gesture that echoes the difference in his attitudes towards his and Veronica's respective sexual histories – the fact that *he* is in another relationship does not seem to offer any such barrier. Dante places a great deal of emphasis on the fact that Caitlin has a fiancée, presumably to distinguish that role from the lesser commitment he feels to his un-affianced girlfriend. However, Caitlin's response here is revealing: 'I offer you my body, and you offer me semantics?'

If there is another critical parallel that one can draw between Veronica and Caitlin, it is again that the women are active, and Dante is passive in both relationships. Much as it is Veronica who returns to the store and fixes their relationship, it is Caitlin who arrives where he is because she knows that he will be struggling with the news that she is engaged. In both situations, Dante is inclined to sit and dwell on both his relationships and his social position – even though he has been equally willing to leave the store to attend a wake and to play hockey on the roof. One cannot, therefore, simply say that he is inactive because his job prevents him from making changes to his situation, as he is willing to disregard the strictures of the workplace when they do not suit him. In this case, the relationship between the two is clear: Caitlin coming to see him makes him happy. He stops caring about being fined and abandons his previous philosophy, telling Randal that this is his 'way of spitting water at life.' Nevertheless, for all the agency this implies, it is Caitlin's activity that causes this change in attitude, rather than anything *he* has done himself.

However, Caitlin is treated a lot less kindly by the film's narrative arc than Veronica. She is the victim of one of the moments that, along with Randal knocking over the casket, would have been a significant moment of slapstick had it been shown onscreen. At one point, having agreed to reunite with Dante, Caitlin goes to the bathroom where the lights do not work and believing Dante is in there, proceeds to have sex with him. Unfortunately for her, this is not Dante but the older man who had earlier conned Dante out of the expensive toilet roll and the pornographic magazine. When Caitlin returns from the bathroom and finds Dante, the situation resolves itself. We learn that the elderly gentleman had been masturbating in the toilet and had died during the act. Caitlin had discovered him (improbably still erect, one might think) and, in the dark, had sex with his corpse. Though the film presents this scene as dark comedy, Caitlin is virtually catatonic after these events. Veronica's sexual history never really hurts her, other than the friction it causes between her and Dante, but Caitlin pays a higher price for transgressing perceived sexual norms for women. This catatonic state is not merely temporary, either, as later instalments in the View Askewniverse suggest that she spends several years in a mental institution because of the event.[1]

Clerks and the relationships between young men

Whatever one might make of Dante's relationships with Veronica and Caitlin, both are of less significance than his relationship with Randal. To understand this relationship, one must first think of the kind of masculinity encountered in the character of Randal. Soles posits the existence of a binary in Smith's films, with his pairs of male protagonists always dividing into a 'geek' and a 'slacker.' The former is essentially industrious and has a desire to thrive (albeit often in various subcultural channels). On the other hand:

> Never far from the creative, artificially foolish geek is his clownish slacker buddy, a natural fool who resists productivity and earnest emotional engagement for fear of appearing uncool in the ironic, postmodern period in which he lives. Cynical, snarky, and comedic in the extreme, the true slacker includes all of Smith's films' buddy sidekicks, such as Randal, Banky, and most famously, Silent Bob's 'heterosexual life mate' Jay.
>
> (Soles 2008: 11)

This dichotomy is an intriguing way of thinking about the relationship between the two characters. However, one must still factor in that Randal is no less creative or geeky than Dante. Nonetheless, Randal stands apart from Dante in one fundamental aspect, which is that he cuts a much less frustrated figure. While Dante hates his job and his position in life, Randal is much more content and is both able and willing to make his condition work for him. Ultimately, we might conclude that *Clerks*, with its twin protagonists fits, more with Greven's idea of films 'that may be said to literalize or allegorize [a] narcissism/masochism split,' even as it continues to draw from the well of the 'buddy film' (Greven 2009: 125). In line with this split, Randal's opposition to social values that demand he acts a certain way fits him much more comfortably than Dante's half-hearted accommodation of those same values. In this way, Randal is a much more Romantic figure – which, indeed, is probably the reason that he gets so many of the film's best lines. The film often translates this Romanticism in masculine terms, perhaps predictably given the history of American Romanticism that saw 'authors such as James Fenimore Cooper, Edgar Allan Poe, and Herman Melville [...] centred on movement away from civilization, "romancing" a vision of U.S. culture free from [...] the feminine disciplinary sphere' (Freeman 2002: 41). For example, when Randal compliments Dante for his 'blatant disregard of store policy,' he frames it as 'one of the ballsiest moves' he has seen. One might easily infer, then, that Randal views his own indifference to rules imposed on him by others as a similarly 'ballsy' stance with all the connotations that such a physical metaphor implies. In Randal's comment that 'my mom has been fucking a dead guy for thirty years. I call him dad,' we see masculinity linked with rebellion; a link is also drawn between masculinity and the generational conflict between Generation X and the Baby Boomers. In this moment, one might also look beyond the explicitly sexual content and detect the familiar figure of the father absent 'by reason of work or business obligations or otherwise as a result of the increase in the breakdown of marriages' (Chopra-Gant 2012: 88).

This comment by Randal, crass as it is, is indicative of the frank discussions of sex that Randal engages in throughout the film. In earlier scenes, Dante was happy to discuss sex (and his own sex life) in front of customers with Veronica. However, Randal talks so much more graphically that even Dante occasionally becomes uncomfortable. Dante acting like his friend in the scene where Randal runs through a laundry list of pornographic titles in front of a mother and her child is unthinkable. In short, Randal is uninhibited, and that extends to the range of sexual practices that he engages in and talks about. This trait in Smith's films had led Soles to suggest 'The slacker sidekick clings to classic masculinity but queers this masculinity through his over-obsession with sex: his sexuality is excessive and spills over the boundaries of the heterosexual, into the "deviant" or queer' (Soles 2008: 5).

While the idea that Randal is representing classic masculinity threatens to elide any number of masculine shades – he ultimately still has more in common with Dante than with Rick Derris – the observation that Randal's sexuality moves into the realm of 'queer' certainly seems to be sound. A vital manifestation of that is his interest in renting hermaphroditic pornography – 'chicks with dicks,' as he calls it, or 'stars with both organs.' As mentioned in Chapter 3, Randal rents this with the idea that he and Dante can watch together, which does little to remove the queer dimension of the activity. The liminality of the hermaphrodite sits well with Randal, a character who is not openly gay but who, later in the film, admits that he does not 'know one thing about chicks.' Whether or not this is a true expression of Randal's sexuality, and whether he is either asexual or displaying signs of something more akin to pansexuality, is never really reconciled. Randal reflects a trend in contemporary Hollywood filmmaking where 'it's not that queers are being explicitly represented; it's that representation has turned queer' (Dreven 2009: 6). Indeed, Randal's sexuality is never defined in anything like explicit terms.

He does, though, present himself as if he is more sexually open than Dante. This is never clearer than in the conversation in the car on the way to the wake of Dante's ex-girlfriend. It is one of the most revealing scenes for thinking about how men use sexual conversation to interact with one another. Randal tells the story of how his cousin broke his neck, attempting to perform oral sex on himself. Dante is disbelieving at first, but the conversation soon turns to whether they, too, have attempted *autofellatio*. Dante denies it, though Randal is now the disbelieving one, calling Dante 'repressed' because he will not admit to it. They comment admiringly about the cousin being able to do it ('but at what cost') before Dante says, 'I could never reach.' However, on this admission, Randal turns on a sixpence and, having acted as if attempting this was commonplace, now calls Dante a pervert (an exact inversion of his earlier statement). This volte-face amounts to a game, a confidence trick of sorts, only rather than robbing Dante of his cash, the end goal of this trick is to impugn his masculinity. It seems that even within this subculture, and even amongst characters who are themselves noticeably queer, some form of homophobia – or, at the very least, the policing of acceptable sexual practice – figures in the interaction between young men. Later in the film, Randal says that his theory is that Dante suffers from 'latent homosexuality.'

Though Randal appears less conservative than Dante, it is also true that when the topic of two men they knew from school living together comes up, it is the latter who says 'It takes different strokes to move the world.' Conversely, Randal uses it as a chance to attack Caitlin: 'In light of this lurid tale, I don't see how you could even romanticize your relationship with Caitlin – she broke your heart and inadvertently drove men to deviant lifestyles.' One should say, though, that a note of caution is needed here because the general tone of Randal's dialogue forces the spectator to question how seriously they should take his words, something reinforced by the potentially queer nature of his own sexuality. In the same conversation, Randal confesses that 'People say crazy shit during sex. One time, I called this girl "Mom,"' a line that either acts purely as a joke or reveals potentially incestuous leanings but either way acts to undercut the seriousness with which he might charge others with deviance.

Regardless, it is undeniable that there is a robust homosocial bond between the two male protagonists that extends far beyond either of Dante's relationships with the two women. It is rather revealing that Dante spends much of the film weighing up the two relationships he has with women to determine which will most benefit him but his complaints about Randal never really lead anywhere. Indeed, it is almost unimaginable that they even could. Dante is more committed to this friendship than to either of the women in his life, and this commitment is reciprocated. Near the end of the film there is a clear change in Randal's behaviour as he moves from goading Dante, both embarrassing and manipulating him throughout the film, towards displaying far more care and consideration. He tells Caitlin that if she hurts him again, he will kill her. Leaving aside the potential violence against a woman such a remark implies (and indeed, Caitlin herself seems not to take the threat seriously), she observes, correctly, that he has always been very protective of Dante. Randal plays this down, remarking instead that this is a question of 'territoriality. He was mine first.' Nevertheless, the film as a whole gives the impression that Randal is deflecting here and that Caitlin perceives their relationship quite clearly. Though the two men trash the store in a fight at the film's climax (to the soundtrack of the band Corrosion of Conformity), this only serves to clear the air between them. They end perhaps even better friends than they began. Viewers alert to the homoerotic charge in much of their interaction may see in this fight 'the violent spectacle that ironically sometimes allows key moments of physical contact between the male pair' (Wyatt 2001: 53).

Of course, Dante and Randal are not the only two male characters in the film. The most famous characters in the View Askewniverse are probably Jay and Silent Bob. The first time that we encounter them, they take up their station outside the video store, and it later becomes clear this is a location where they sell drugs. From the first time the audience sees these characters, Jay conveys a distinctive type of masculinity as, with no prompting from any other character or stimulus, his first act is to shout, 'we need some tits and ass!' He follows this by throwing punches out into the empty air, again with little rhyme or reason (see Figure 5.3). Once Jay starts talking in more

Figure 5.3 Jay and Silent Bob – Jay throws punches to the air.

earnest – it would be a mistake to suggest what he has with the aptly named Silent Bob constitutes a conversation – he turns for a second to the subject of how they will survive. His suggestion is they will make some money today, before he again turns towards his libido: 'We're going to go to that party and get some pussy! I'm gonna fuck this bitch, that bitch [...] I'LL FUCK ANYTHING THAT MOVES!,' The last exclamation is a reference to Dennis Hopper's character Frank Booth in *Blue Velvet* (Lynch, 1986). Bob draws his attention back to the real world, and Jay's reaction is to immediately start threatening another man who is nearby. Jay's comment to Silent Bob after the fact is pointlessly gratuitous: 'you and me are going to cut off that fucker's head, and take out his fucking soul!' – the kind of threat made ridiculous by the very impossibility of delivering on it. This kind of excessive, even overbearing masculinity that colours every gesture extends throughout the film. When playing hockey, Dante calls down to ask if there are any balls down there. Jay, predictably and without a hint of irony, shouts back up something about the biggest pair you have ever seen, a crude statement about his testicular endowment.

Much like Randal, Jay's sexuality is so excessive that it spills over the boundaries of accepted heteronormativity into the realm of the queer. One monologue delivered at Silent Bob is particularly revealing: 'Damn Silent Bob! You one rude motherfucker! But you're cute as hell. I wanna go down on you and suckle you. And then, I wanna line up three more guys, and make like a circus seal [...] ewww! You fucking faggot! I fucking hate guys! I LOVE WOMEN!' Jay supplements this diatribe with actions such as bobbing his head, mimicking the performance of the act itself, before jumping up when the homophobic impulse kicks in. Later, Jay talks about Caitlin and how he would like to have sex with her but again finds himself simulating sex towards Silent Bob in order to demonstrate this, and one might start to wonder exactly how far this misdirected lust might extend. Jay's deviant sexuality, though, goes beyond any potential interest in men, as shown by his comment 'I don't care if she is my cousin or not, I'm gonna knock those boots again tonight.' Jay is loud, obnoxious, and potentially untrustworthy, both because of his *braggadocio* and because we see him both selling drugs and lying in the film. Jay lies right to Dante's face – he says he has not been dealing drugs in front of the store, but a second later someone attempts to buy drugs, and he immediately begins trying to sell with Dante still there. However, whether one takes his comments at face value or not, having both Jay and Randal engage in this kind of language implies that this is not unique to Randal but rather a mode of discourse that runs deep throughout the young men of this subculture.

Jay is a ridiculous character, little more than a man-child, but Jay is also the one who starts to spell things out for Dante. He talks to Dante about what his plans are regarding Caitlin and Veronica and notes that while Caitlin is crazy, he often sees Veronica doing things for Dante, things that he does not appreciate enough if it takes Jay (of all people) to point them out. Jay is predictably unable to put this into words with any eloquence, so it falls to Silent Bob (Smith), with his one line in the movie, to spell things out: 'there's a million fine looking women in the world, but they don't all bring you lasagne at work. Most of them just cheat on you.' Misogyny aside, this prompts a moment of epiphany for Dante. Unfortunately for him, right at this moment, Randal is telling Veronica that Dante does not love her and that he will be returning to his relationship with Caitlin, because, as Randal later explains 'I thought I was doing you a favour. You're always saying how you can't initiate change yourself; I thought I'd give you a hand.' Perhaps naturally, Veronica tells Dante off, ignoring his protestations of love and declaring that she wants him to follow through and live with the consequences of his idiocy. However, again this is tied to his masculinity: 'Randal had the balls to tell me [...] and having him do it was the weakest move ever, you're spineless.' In fact, Dante had nothing to do with Randal telling Veronica about Caitlin, but the trope that seems to recur in Dante's bad day is that when things go wrong, they almost always seem to involve his masculinity. He is either powerless to deal with problems or others question his manhood or backbone. For those in Generation X who do not conform to hegemonic expectations of masculinity, how to be a man in this world seems to be just as fraught as their economic situation as young Americans.

Note

1 In *Chasing Amy* (1997), Alyssa Jones reveals that Caitlin is committed after the incident. The audience sees Caitlin in institution in the comic book, *Clerks: The Holiday Special* (1998).

Conclusion

Clerks launched not just the directorial career of Kevin Smith but also his View Askewniverse. Taking its name from Smith and producer Scott Mosier's company View Askew Productions, the View Askewniverse represents the cinematic world portrayed in Smith's film, a world that is connected through characters, storylines, locations, and even actors who have repeatedly featured in Smith's films. With each successive Smith film making several references to his previous efforts, the View Askewniverse has continued to expand and evolve, becoming a staple of popular (sub)culture and demanding of its viewers an in-depth knowledge of Smith's films if they are to understand the nuances of particular narrative information. Greater familiarity with the existing instalments can therefore enhance viewers' appreciation of films that can also stand as self-contained narratives.

Clerks established quite a few staples of the View Askewniverse: the Quick Stop, Dante and Randall, Jay and Silent Bob, and secondary characters like Caitlin Bree and Rick Derris. Even events that only feature briefly in the film like the wake of July Dwyer resurface in other films. Sometimes these are mentioned in conversation by newly introduced characters while at other times the same actors make cameo appearances playing different characters (such as Brian O'Halloran's brief appearances in *Mallrats* [1995], *Chasing Amy* [1997], and *Dogma* [1999]). By the time Smith made his fifth contribution to this universe, *Jay and Silent Bob Strike Back* (2001), the fictional world in his films had expanded to such an extent that only a very particular demographic – Smith's hardcore fans – would be able to understand all nuances and permutations. As Roger Ebert put it in his review: 'Whether you will like "Jay and Silent Bob" depends on who you are. Most movies are made for everybody. Kevin Smith's movies are either made specifically for you, or specifically not made for you' (Ebert, 2001). By that time, the generational conflict of his earlier films may have been relegated to the past, but even though Smith himself was now in his

Conclusion   93

thirties, subcultural attitudes and affinities formed when both the filmmaker and his audience were young still carried significant weight.

At the end of *Jay and Silent Bob Strike Back*, reprising her role as God after having played the deity in *Dogma*, Alannis Morissette is seen to close the fictional Askewniverse book, playfully implying that there will be no more films with storylines taking place in this fictional world. Smith had implied as much, motivated in large part by Jason Mewes' troubles with heroin addiction. However, following the commercially unsuccessfully and critically panned *Jersey Girl* (2004), a feature that had no connection to the Askewniverse, and with a cleaned-up Mewes in tow, in 2006 Smith decided to make a sequel to *Clerks*, showing the continuing significance of his debut feature and the ongoing interest in the film, as well as of its place in the now substantially expanded View Askewniverse. Originally to be called *The Passion of the Clerks* (a play on *The Passion of the Christ* [Gibson, 2004]) the film was eventually – sensibly – retitled more simply just as *Clerks II*.

The sequel begins with Dante arriving at the Quick Stop to find the store on fire and the revelation that Randal is responsible since he has (once again) left the coffee pot on when he left the previous night. We then fast forward to the two working at a fast food restaurant on what is Dante's last day. Quite literally, then, in the intervening years (and despite the first film ending with the message that Dante was going to get his life together) the two have risen no further in the hierarchy of the service sector and are now working in the original 'McJobs.' Randal's boss, Becky Scott (Rosario Dawson), even references the term directly, taunting him: 'The smartest of smart asses got rattled by some fucking loser coming in here giving you shit about your McJob.'

But though the location has changed, there are many continuities between the sequel and the original film. Dante finds himself in a love triangle with two women, the aforementioned Becky and his fiancée Emma Bunting (Jennifer Schwalbach), with whom he plans to leave for Florida after this final day at Mooby's restaurant. Dante hides from his job by painting Becky's nails, echoing the scene from the first film where he paints Veronica's nails behind the store counter. Jay and Silent Bob continue to sell drugs and hang around outside, with Jay performing his strange dances in between sales. Randal continues to discuss popular culture in the workplace, this time getting into a debate with younger staff and customers of the restaurant as to the respective merits of the *Star Wars* and *Lord of the Rings* franchises, insisting 'All right, look, there's only one Return, okay, and it ain't of the king [...] it's of the Jedi.' He mocks the *Lord of the Rings* trilogy, implying that a gay sex scene between Frodo and Samwise would have been the more appropriate ending for *Return of the King*.

However, explicit dialogue aside, the most significant part of this exchange is the younger cashier saying to a sympathetic customer, 'you'll have to excuse him – he's not "down" with the trilogy.' Whatever subcultural capital Randal retains, it is no longer part of a youth culture. That mantle has been passed on, and Randal and his interests look particularly dated. Where there is generational conflict, it is not between Generation X and the Baby Boomers; antagonism is now directed towards those in the Millennial demographic. Randal usually dominates these exchanges with younger co-workers, but then this is a film for people who are now in their thirties and who have grown up with the View Askewniverse. That this is a fantasy in which they get the better in all exchanges is no surprise. Additional references to other films come thick and fast for the fans of Smith's work, not least through the characters of Jay and Silent Bob who reference films from the youth of this generation such as *Full Metal Jacket* (Kubrick, 1987) and *The Silence of the Lambs* (Demme, 1991).

Randal's inappropriate talk in front of customers is reproduced, with the shift being that instead of talking about sex and pornography he talks about (and uses) ethnic slurs and discusses the disabled. The two protagonists once again leave their place of work and go driving, only in this incarnation it is *Randal* who needs to escape, and the two leave the restaurant to go karting together. At this point, the soundtrack features 'Raindrops Keep Falling on My Head,' harking back to the relationship between the title characters in the film *Butch Cassidy and the Sundance Kid* (Hill, 1969). The sequel also reproduces Randal's deviant sexuality of the first film, only this time his fascination is not with trans pornography but with bestiality (or, as one character repeatedly insists on calling it, 'interspecies erotica'). This preoccupation leads to a central set piece of sexually inflected humour, with the off-screen relations with a corpse displaced in favour of a sex show featuring a man and a donkey. While it is natural enough that this act is not filmed in any close detail, it is something that viewers are 'shown,' rather than 'told,' as was the case with the original *Clerks*. For that alone, the sequel pushes the boundaries of taste far more than the original movie.

Finally, the film reaches a climax with a shouting match between Dante and Randal once they have been jailed along with Jay and Silent Bob. This time, though, Dante lands as many telling verbal blows as Randal, their dialogue being much more even-handed. In the sequel, Randal cuts a much less confident figure. Though he talks in much the same fashion, he is less assured and demonstrates more vulnerability. The more astute philosophical observations that had been his forte in 1994 tend to now come from other characters. At one point, Randal says that 'sometimes I get the feeling the world kind of left us behind a long time ago.' In the end, though, he does come up with the idea that saves their friendship: that Dante should stay in New Jersey and they should buy the Quick Stop and reopen it together. Though they lack the necessary financial resources, Jay and Silent Bob can lend them money (from the royalties they acquire at the end of *Jay and Silent Bob Strike Back*), and the two are able to make Randal's vision a reality. Dante stays in New Jersey rather than moving to Florida and marries Becky instead of Emma, and the film finishes with a slow pullback from the two clerks behind the Quick Stop counter as the colour of the film fades to the black and white of the original, to the familiar sound of Soul Asylum. In the very last seconds, Smith's mother reprises her role as the milkmaid, sat on the floor surrounded by cartons.

    The introduction to this volume outlined that the first film received praise for its authenticity. The ending of *Clerks II*, however, is not close to anything relating to real experience. If viewers were first attracted by *Clerks'* naturalism, this ending would undoubtedly ring hollow. Jay and Silent Bob having the money to lend Dante and Randal at the exact moment they need it and being willing to do so serves as an unconvincing *deus ex machina* in order to end the film with an image that Smith had been living with since before *Jay and Silent Bob Strike Back*. But to ask for naturalism would be to miss the point. The ending (and in many ways, the whole film) offers a fantasy of complete withdrawal into the past. *Clerks II* is not a youth film, but like the rest of the View Askewniverse, it was made primarily for the people who watched the first film and who, crucially, grew up with the rest of the movies. These people are envisaged, much like the characters onscreen, to be approaching or over thirty by the time that Smith made the film. The soundtrack features not the alternative music of 2006 but music from acts like Talking Heads, Alanis Morrisette, and Smashing Pumpkins – bands and acts with independent and alternative credentials but very much established. On the other hand, these are also artists that refer back to Smith's adolescence and to the time of *Clerks* and *Chasing Amy*, rather than bands especially popular with young audiences at the time of filming. Little personal growth is evident in the decision of the characters to work in the store forever. Owning the store feels like a means to an end, a way of getting to hang out with your buddy for the rest of your life, rather than as a genuine ambition for either character. The fade to black and white underneath a song from the original film is a retreat from the pressures of the world rather than a way of dealing with them. Here, cinema makes that kind of pleasant haven possible in a way that no living, embodied thirty-year-old could ever successfully realise.

    Fifteen years after *Clerks II*, the View Askewniverse does not look as if it is going to disappear any time soon, and despite repeatedly suggesting that he will leave either the entire universe or specific characters behind, Smith seems to be repeatedly drawn back to this fictional world. Six years after *Jay and Silent Bob's Groovy Cartoon Movie* (Smith, 2013), Mewes and Smith reprised their roles as the title characters in *Jay and Silent Bob Reboot* (Smith, 2019). Here, the film parodies the recent trend in comic book movies to reboot films oriented around beloved characters in order to remake commercially reliable ventures. Smith achieves this by effectively borrowing the plot of *Jay and Silent Bob Strike Back* and changing plot details so that the reason for their journey is now a studio reboot of the 'Bluntman and Chronic' series. Though a commercial failure that lost around $5m at the box office, viewers of *Clerks* will have been interested in the film's revelation that all along, it has been Jay and Silent Bob who have been jamming the store's shutters with gum.

At the time of writing, Smith has spoken about working on sequels to both *Mallrats* and *Clerks*.[1] If these films are ever made, they will become the ninth and tenth films in the View Askewniverse (although this number may vary as Smith also claims that his 2008 film, *Zack and Miri Make a Porno*, was subsequently ret-conned into this fictional universe by *Jay and Silent Bob Reboot*).[2] More than that, however, they will become part of a diverse fictional world relayed across a variety of media platforms. In addition to the feature films, a short-lived animated series and a computer game have both been set in this world, while at the time of writing STX Entertainment are working on bringing Jay and Silent Bob into the world of virtual reality. The affection that people have for these characters becomes clear when one looks at the way that they have continued to reappear in cinema and other media. The video game *Jay and Silent Bob Chronic Blunt Punch* was even financed as a result of a successful crowdfunding campaign. When looked at altogether, the loyalty that fans have had to Smith's creation across two and a half decades demonstrates that *Clerks* connected with a youth audience so strongly that it has powered a series of films and related media which are now, necessarily, far removed from the independent status of the original but which still maintain a distinctive, not quite homogenised position in the cultural landscape. Though this volume ends here, as long as that endures, 'God' may not be called upon to close the book on the View Askewniverse a second time for many years to come.

Clerks II brings to a symbolic end a journey through the View Askewniverse that began in 1994. As I mentioned above, Smith would again revisit that universe with *Jay and Silent Bob Reboot* (2019), but nevertheless, there is a certain amount of closure at the end of *Clerks II*. The journey from the first film to the end of its sequel and the similarities and differences between the two films tell us that the cultural dispositions

Conclusion 97

that we acquire in our youth are not simply passing fancies; they have a lasting effect on us. Not everyone who watched *Clerks* became full-fledged fans of Kevin Smith, but many of a certain age (and with shared interests) did. What is clear is that, even as generational antagonisms shift or fade, continuities in humour, discourse, and taste persist into adulthood. We all age, but one never *completely* outgrows the subcultures of our formative years.

This, then, speaks to an ongoing relevance for films like *Clerks* and their importance in youth culture, far beyond the early 1990s. There are, though, particularly significant local factors about that period and about youth cinema that *Clerks* reveals, as this volume has tried to demonstrate. *Clerks* tells us that a crucial aspect of youth cinema is that it is produced *by* the young and not simply *for* the young. It is imperative that the film speaks with an authentic voice, one actually of the subculture and able to understand and articulate its worldview. In this case, the success of the film was the result of it being made without corporate interference by a young person who had worked in this kind of job. In addition, Smith was clearly knowledgeable about cultural reference points like *Star Wars*. The interest in the film stems in large part from the fact that Smith offers a perspective on America at this time, on the job market, and on working in the service industry, that his peers could see as somehow speaking for them.

In doing so, the film articulates several things about Generation X. Members of this cohort were accused of aimlessness by their elders, but while Dante seems to suffer with that for much of the film, in truth their lack of drive stems more from other factors. The game of life was rigged against them by the corporate world, a world which, in turn, is inauthentic and hollow. Engagement with such a world would crush one's spirit since people cannot operate within it and retain their independence simultaneously. The young men of this generation were not simply apathetic, *Clerks* seems to say, but intelligent, passionate, and at times uncertain – ultimately too Romantic for their own good. There is clearly something Romantic about the fraternal bonds of Dante and Randal and Jay and Silent Bob, homosocial friendships that run deeper than any of the relationships the characters have with women. More than that, though, their alternative subcultures place so much value on their individuality that they are not willing to compromise it by 'selling out.' Kevin Smith, of course, escaped this dilemma by becoming a filmmaker (mostly working within independent structures but also doing a film for a studio and even acting in big action films like *Die Hard 4.0* (Wiseman, 2007) – and therefore occasionally 'selling out'). However, his protagonists, like the majority in this grouping, were not as fortunate, and so the improbable ending to the sequel offers a semblance of a happy ending without Dante and Randal having to make that kind of compromise. In the end, this is part of the fantasy, because they too were more fortunate than most of the audience.

Notes

1 For *Clerks 3*, see Garvey (2019). For *Mallrats 2*, see Alexander (2020).
2 Smith explained this in a 2019 video for *Vanity Fair*: https://www.youtube.com/watch?v=9Rvpo6NEkBY

Bibliography

Alexander, S. (2020) 'Ben Affleck Confirmed Returning to Mallrats 2, According to Kevin Smith', *Digital Spy*, online, 13 August, https://www.digitalspy.com/movies/a33595106/ben-affleck-mallrats-2-kevin-smith/.

Alsen, E. (1996) *Romantic Postmodernism in American Fiction*, Atlanta, GA: Rodopi.

Amago, S. (2007) 'Can Anyone Rock Like We Do? Or, How the Gen X Aesthetic Transcends the Age of the Writer', in C. Henseler and R.D. Pope (eds) *Generation X Rocks: Contemporary Peninsular Fiction, Film, and Rock Culture*, Nashville, TN: Vanderbilt University Press, pp. 59–77.

Baudrillard, J. (1994) *Simulacra and Simulation*, Ann Arbor, MI: University of Michigan Press (Translated from French by Sheila Faria Glaser).

Baudrillard, J. (2017) *Symbolic Exchange and Death*, London: Sage (Translated from French by Iain Hamilton Grant).

Best, S. and Kellner, D. (1997) *The Postmodern Turn*, New York: Guildford Press.

Bourdieu, P. (1994) *Distinction: A Social Critique of the Judgement of Taste*, London: Routledge (Translated from French by Richard Nice).

Brickman, Barbara Jane (2018) *Grease: Gender, Nostalgia and Youth Consumption in the Blockbuster Era*, London: Routledge.

Brock, W.E. (1987) 'They're not "McJobs"', *Washington Post*, online, 11 June, https://www.washingtonpost.com/archive/opinions/1987/06/11/theyre-not-mcjobs/7bcd8610-796f-4698-a761-7b4155e8c33d/.

Buckingham, D. (2013) *After the Death of Childhood: Growing Up in the Age of Electronic Media*, Cambridge: Polity.

Carroll, T. (2003) 'Talking Out of School: Academia Meets Generation X', in J.M. Ulrich and A.L. Harris (eds) *GenXegesis: Essays on Alternative Youth (Sub)culture*, Madison, WI: University of Wisconsin Press, pp. 199–220.

Chopra-Gant, M. (2012) '"I'd Fight My Dad": Absent Fathers and Mediated Masculinities in *Fight Club*', in T. Shary (ed) *Millennial Masculinity: Men in Contemporary American Cinema*, Detroit: Wayne State University Press, pp. 85–100.

Bibliography

Clover, J. (2009) *1989: Bob Dylan Didn't Have This to Sing About*, Oakland, CA: University of California Press.

Coupland, D. (1991) *Generation X: Tales for an Accelerated Culture*, New York: St. Martin's Press.

Davis, C. (2018) 'Emerson's Telescope: Jones Very and Romantic Individualism', *New England Quarterly*, Vol. 91, No. 3, pp. 483–507.

Davies, P.J. and Wells, P. (2002) *American Film and Politics from Reagan to Bush Jr.*, Manchester: Manchester University Press.

De Beauvoir, S. (1997) *The Second Sex*, London: Vintage (Translated from French by H.M. Parshley).

De Certeau, M. (1988) *The Practice of Everyday Life*, Berkeley, CA: University of California Press (Translated from French by Steven F. Rendall).

Doherty, T. (2010) *Teenagers and Teenpics: The Juvenilization of American Movies in the 1950s*, Philadelphia, PA: Temple University Press.

Doody, C. (2011) 'X-Plained: The Production and Reception History of Douglas Coupland's Generation X', *Papers of the Bibliographical Society of Canada*, Vol. 49, No. 1, pp. 5–34.

Drury, C. (2005) *Management Accounting for Business*, London: Thomson.

Ebert, R. (1994) '*Clerks* Movie Review & Film Summary', *RogerEbert.com*, online, 4 November, https://www.rogerebert.com/reviews/clerks-1994.

Ebert, R. (1995) '*Mallrats* Movie Review & Film Summary', *RogerEbert.com*, online, 20 October, https://www.rogerebert.com/reviews/mallrats-1995.

Ebert, R. (2001) 'Jay and Silent Bob Strike Back Movie Review & Film Summary' *RogerEbert.com*, online, 24 August, https://www.rogerebert.com/reviews/jay-and-silent-bob-strike-back-2001.

Elliot, F.R. (1996) *Gender, Family & Society*, Basingstoke: MacMillan.

Etzioni, A. (1986) 'The Fast-Food Factories: McJobs Are Bad for Kids', *Washington Post*, online, 24 August, https://www.washingtonpost.com/archive/opinions/1986/08/24/the-fast-food-factories-mcjobs-are-bad-for-kids/b3d7bbeb-5e9a-4335-afdd-2030cb7bc775/.

Fain, G. (1991) *Leisure and Ethics: Reflections on the Philosophy of Leisure*, Washington, DC: American Alliance for Health, Physical Education, Recreation, and Dance; American Association for Leisure and Recreation.

Faludi, S. (2010) *Backlash: The Undeclared War against Women*, London: Vintage.

Field, S. (1997) *The Romance of Desire: Emerson's Commitment to Incompletion*, Madison, NJ: Fairleigh Dickinson University Press.

Fonarow, W. (2006) *Empire of Dirt: The Aesthetics and Rituals of British Indie Music*, Middletown, CT: Wesleyan University Press.

Fraser, J. (1994) 'The Dalai Lama of Generation X', *Saturday Night*, Vol. 109, No. 2, p. 8.

Freedland, J. (1994) 'An Icon of Alienation', *Guardian*, online, 23 April, https://www.theguardian.com/music/from-the-archive-blog/2014/apr/05/kurt-cobain-an-icon-of-alienation.

Freeman, E. (2002) *The Wedding Complex: Forms of Belonging in Modern American Culture*, Durham, NC: Duke University Press.

Garvey, M. (2019) 'Kevin Smith Announces 'Clerks III' Will Be Happening', *CNN*, online, 4 October, https://edition.cnn.com/2019/10/04/entertainment/kevin-smith-clerks-3-trnd/index.html.

Gilmore, M. (2010) *American Romanticism and the Marketplace*, Chicago, IL: University of Chicago Press.

Goodman, E. (1983) 'Fear of Wimphood', *Washington Post*, online, 18 October, https://www.washingtonpost.com/archive/politics/1983/10/18/fear-of-wimphood/b922961e-6ef0-4cb7-8871-1ec2ce4091c6/.

Goodwin, A. (1991) 'Popular Music and Postmodern Theory', *Cultural Studies*, Vol. 5, No. 2, pp. 174–190.

Goulart, R. (1969) *The Assault on Childhood*, Los Angeles, CA: Sherbourne.

Greven, D. (2009) *Manhood in Hollywood from Bush to Bush*, Austin, TX: University of Texas Press.

Grossberg, L. (1992) *We Gotta Get Out of This Place: Popular Conservatism and Postmodern Culture*, New York: Routledge.

Halberstam, J. (2018) *Female Masculinity*, Durham, NC: Duke University Press.

Hall, S. and Jefferson, T. (1976) 'Subcultures, Cultures and Class': A Theoretical Overview', in S. Hall and T. Jefferson (eds) *Resistance through Rituals: Youth Subcultures in Post-War Britain*, London: HarperCollins, pp. 9–74.

Hanson, P. (2002) *The Cinema of Generation X: A Critical Study*, Jefferson, NC: McFarland.

Harrington, M. (1997) *The Other America: Poverty in the United States*, New York: Simon and Schuster.

Hawkins, A.F. (1987) 'McJobs (Cot'd)', *Washington Post*, online, 30 June, https://www.washingtonpost.com/archive/opinions/1987/06/30/mcjobs-contd/8b1c0d54-5c08-4d56-9380-9c7c7a73be18/.

Hebdige, D. (1979) *Subculture: The Meaning of Style*, London: Routledge.

Hebdige, D. (1988) *Hiding in the Light: On Images and Things*, London: Routledge.

Hicks, B. (2009) *Love All the People*, London: Constable.

Hill, D.D. (2007) *As Seen in Vogue: A Century of American Fashion in Advertising*, Lubbock: Texas Tech University Press.

Howe, N. and Strauss, W. (1992) 'The New Generation Gap', *The Atlantic*, Vol. 270, No. 6, pp. 67–89.

'Interview with Kevin Smith' (2001) *Frontline*, online, https://www.pbs.org/wgbh/pages/frontline/shows/hollywood/interviews/smith.html.

Jameson, F. (1991) *Postmodernism: Or, the Cultural Logic of Late Capitalism*, London: Verso.

Jarvis, B. (1998) *Postmodern Cartographies: The Geographical Imagination in Contemporary American Culture*, New York: St. Martin's Press.

Jeffords, S. (1994) *Hard Bodies: Hollywood Masculinity in the Reagan Era*, New Brunswick, NJ: Rutgers University Press.

Jenkins, H. (1992) *Textual Poachers: Television Fans and Participatory Culture*, London: Routledge.

Ki, W. (2003) 'The Post-Romantic Sublime: Generation X and the Intransigence of the Surplus Jouissance', *Working with English: Medieval and Modern Language, Literature and Drama*, No. 1, pp. 16–27.

Bibliography

King, G. (2005) *American Independent Cinema*, London: I.B. Tauris.

King, G. (2013) 'Thriving or in Permanent Crisis? Discourses on the State of Indie Cinema', in G. King, C. Molloy, and Y. Tzioumakis (eds) *American Independent Cinema: Indie, Indiewood and Beyond*, London: Routledge, pp. 41–52.

Kunyosying, K. and Soles, C. (2012) 'Postmodern Geekdom as Simulated Ethnicity', *Jump Cut: A Review of Contemporary Media*, Vol. 54, online, https://www.eju mpcut.org/archive/jc54.2012/SolesKunyoGeedom/index.html.

Latham, R. (2002) *Consuming Youth: Vampires, Cyborgs, & the Culture of Consumption*, Chicago, IL: University of Chicago Press.

Leidl, D. (2013) 'American X: The Ironic History of a Generation', in C. Hensler (ed) *Generation X Goes Global: Mapping a Youth Culture in Motion*, New York: Routledge, pp. xiii–xxiii.

Levy, E. (1999) *Cinema of Outsiders: The Rise of American Independent Film*, New York: New York University Press.

Lohr, S. (1994) 'No More McJobs for Mr. X.', *New York Times*, 29 May, Section 9, p. 2.

Lury, C. (1996) *Consumer Culture*, Cambridge: Polity.

Marin, R. (1992) 'Grunge: A Success Story', *New York Times*, 15 November, Section 9, p. 1.

Mihalic, J. (1984) 'Hair on the President's Chest', *Wall Street Journal*, 11 May, p. 30.

Moore, R. (2010) *Sells Like Teen Spirit: Music, Youth Culture and Social Crisis*, New York: New York University Press.

Muir, J.K. (2012) *An Askew View 2: The Films of Kevin Smith*, Lanham, MD: Rowman and Littlefield.

Nelson, Elissa (2019) *John Hughes, Hollywood, and the Golden Age of Teen Film*, London: Routledge.

Newman, M. (2011) *Indie: An American Film Culture*, New York: Columbia University Press.

Ntarangwi, M. (2013) 'Generation X Meets the Uhuru Generation in East Africa', in C. Henseler (ed) *Generation X Goes Global: Mapping a Youth Culture in Motion*, New York: Routledge, pp. 73–90.

Owen, R. (1999) *Gen X TV: The Brady Bunch to Melrose Place*, Syracuse, NY: Syracuse University Press.

Postman, N. (1982) *The Disappearance of Childhood*, London: Vintage.

Powers, S., Rothman, D. and Rothman, S. (1996) *Hollywood's America: Social and Political Themes in Motion Pictures*, Oxford: Westview.

Primeau, R. (1996) *Romance of the Road: The Literature of the American Highway*, Bowling Green, OH: Bowling Green State University Popular Press.

Reich, R.B. (1985) 'Reagan's Hidden "Industrial Policy"', *New York Times*, 4 August, Section 3, p. 3.

Richie, K. (2002) *Marketing to Generation X*, New York: Free Press.

Riesman, D. (1993) 'Leisure and Work in Postindustrial Society', in *Abundance for What?*, London: Transaction, pp. 162–183.

Rosenthal, B. (1980) *City of Nature: Journeys to Nature in the Age of American Romanticism*, Newark, DE: University of Delaware Press.

Sexton, J. (2017) 'Indie Music Cultures and American Indie Cinema', in G. King (ed) *A Companion to American Indie Film*, Oxford: Wiley-Blackwell, pp. 106–28.

Shary, T. (2012) 'Introduction', in T. Shary (ed) *Millennial Masculinity: Men in Contemporary American Cinema*, Detroit, MI: Wayne State University Press, pp. 1–18.

Shuker, R. (2017) *Popular Music: The Key Concepts*, London: Routledge.

Slater, D. (1998) *Consumer Culture and Modernity*, Cambridge: Polity.

Slocum, J.D. (2005) *Rebel Without a Cause: Approaches to a Maverick Masterwork*, Albany, NY: State University of New York Press.

Smith, A.C., Blackwell, T. and Immirzi, E. (1975) *Paper Voices*, London: Chatto and Windus.

Soles, C.M. (2008) *Falling Out of the Closet: Kevin Smith, Queerness, and Independent Film*, Unpublished PhD Thesis, University of Oregon.

Stacey, J. (1996) *In the Name of the Family: Rethinking Family Values in the Postmodern Age*, Boston, MA: Beacon.

Sten, C. (1974) 'Bartleby the Transcendentalist: Melville's Dead Letter to Emerson', *Modern Language Quarterly*, Vol. 35, No. 1, pp. 30–44.

Strong, C. (2017) *Grunge: Music and Memory*, Farnham: Ashgate.

Taylor, A. (2012) 'Adam Sandler, an Apologia: Anger, Arrested Adolescence, *Amour Fou*', in T. Shary (ed) *Millennial Masculinity: Men in Contemporary American Cinema*, Detroit, MI: Wayne State University Press, pp. 19–51.

'The Myth of "McJobs,"' (1987) *National Review*, 10 April, pp. 19–20.

Thoreau, H.D. (1997) *Walden*, Boston, MA: Beacon (Introduction by Bill McKibben).

Thornton, S. (1996) *Club Cultures: Music, Media and Subcultural Capital*, Middletown, CT: Wesleyan University Press.

Tropiano, S. (2006) *Rebels & Chicks: A History of the Hollywood Teen Movie*, New York: Backstage.

Tzioumakis, Y. (2006) *American Independent Cinema: An Introduction*, Edinburgh: Edinburgh University Press.

Veblen, T. (1994) *The Theory of the Leisure Class*, London: Penguin (Introduction by R. Lekachman).

Williams, R. (1977) *Marxism and Literature*, Oxford: Oxford University Press.

Woodward, B. (1994) *The Agenda: Inside the Clinton White House*, New York: Simon and Schuster.

Wyatt, J. (2001) 'Identity, Queerness and Homosocial Bonding: The Case of *Swingers*', in P. Lehman (ed) *Masculinity: Bodies, Movies, Culture*, New York: Routledge, pp. 51–66.

Zustiak, G.B. (1996) *The Next Generation: Understanding and Meeting the Needs of Generation X*, Joplin, MO: College Press.

Index

Alice in Chains 18, 19, 22
alpha male 81–84
Anderson, Jeff 5, 8, 38, 67
anti-sabbatical 41
arthouse 8–10
authenticity 1–4, 15–16, 19–22, 41, 84, 95, 97

Babenko, Héctor 77
Baby Boomers 2, 12–13, 59, 87, 94
Backlash sentiment 74
Bad Religion 53
Baudrillard, Jean 14, 29
bestiality 94
Bill Haley and His Comets 57
Bird 77
Blue Velvet 90
Bourdieu, Pierre 9, 17, 49
Brando, Marlon 57
Bree, Caitlin 7, 78, 84–91
Brock, Bill 27
Bush, George H.W. 11, 27, 77
Butch Cassidy and the Sundance Kid 94

capitalism, 20–21, 30, 32, 42, 45–46, 60, 63
Chasing Amy, 6, 57, 77, 92, 95
cigarettes 34, 36, 61–62, 71, 79
Clerks II 93–96
Clinton, Bill 27–28, 74–75
Cobain, Kurt 16–17, 22, 25–26, 28, 77
consumer culture 5, 24, 32, 50, 56–72
Corrosion of Conformity, 89
Coupland, Douglas 4, 11, 37; and consumption 42–43; and

employment 28–32; and Life as Experiences 41–43
cultural capital 41, 67–72, 94
customers 5, 34–39, 43, 45–48, 54, 61, 67–68; as problematic 34–36, 61–66, 78

dance music 20
Dawson, Rosario 93
de Certeau, Michel 40, 44–48, 55
Derris, Rick 78–79, 87, 92
divorce 10, 12–13, 74
Dogma 6, 92–93

Eastwood, Clint 77
Ebert, Roger 1–2, 92
eggs 38, 64–65
Emerson, Ralph Waldo 42

Fight Club see Fincher, David
Filmmaker magazine, 8
Fincher, David 15

Gatorade 61
generational conflict 33–34, 87, 92, 94
Generation X, 1–4, 10–18, 43, 49, 63; and apathy 11–12; and employment 24–39, 40–43; and masculinity 78, 87, 91; and race 11–12
Ghigliotti, Marilyn *see* Loughran, Veronica
glam metal 4, 16, 77
Graves, Randal 5–6, 8, 17, 33–35, 38–39, 53–55, 60–61, 84–85, 90–91, 97–98; and *Clerks II* 93–95;

and Consumer culture 63–67; and Cultural Capital 67–72; and Insubordination 36–37, 45–48; and sex 86–89; and *Star Wars* 49–52
grunge 4, 11, 16–22, 25, 28–29, 32; and Consumer culture 63, 70; and masculinity 77–78
guidance counsellor 38–39, 64

Hawkins, Augustus 27
Hicks, Dante 5–7, 17, 22, 53–55, 68, 70–71, 92–95, 97–98; and Consumer culture 60–66; and employment 32–37; and masculinity 78–91; and slacking 43–48; and *Star Wars* 49–52, 70
hockey 5, 33, 43–45, 54, 61, 85, 90
Hogan, Hulk 76–77
hypermasculinity 76–77

Independent cinema, 1–2, 4, 19, 21, 81; and authenticity 1–3; and Cultural capital 67–72; and masculinity 76–77; and opposition to Hollywood 7–10
Indiana Jones and The Temple of Doom 35, 70
indie music 18–20
irony 8, 15–17, 29, 32, 38, 43, 59, 70, 86, 89–90

Jarmusch, Jim 8–10
Jaws 70
Jay 6, 61, 70, 86, 92–97; and masculinity 89–91
Jay and Silent Bob Strike Back 92–93, 95–96
Jersey Girl 93
The Jesus Lizard 44

Kerouac, Jack 12, 28, 32
Kiss of the Spider Woman 77
Kubrick, Stanley 94

leisure class 40, 68
Linklater, Richard 2–3, 28, 50
Lord of the Rings 93
Loughran, Veronica 5, 7, 43, 62, 84–87, 91, 93; as action hero 79–80; and Dante 79–84

Love Among Freaks 22
Lucas, George 14, 52
Lynch, David 14–15, 90

Mallrats 77, 92, 96
masturbation 38–39, 63–64, 85
McJobs 4–5, 26–30, 93
Melville, Herman 31, 86
Mewes, Jason 93, 96
milkmaids 65–66, 95
Miramax, 1, 8–9, 22

Navy SEALS 68–69
neo-liberalism 26, 58
New York Times 27–28
nihilism 13, 29, 43
Nixon, Richard 11

Office Space, 56
O'Halloran, Brian 5, 92
oral sex 6, 82–83, 88

pornography 6, 48, 63, 66–67, 85, 87, 94
postindustrial 26, 40–41, 58, 73
Poverty Jet Set 41
Pulp Fiction 1
punk 4, 16–17, 20, 22, 28, 53

queer 78, 83, 87–88, 90

Reagan, Ronald 11, 25–28, 73–76
Reaganomics 26, 58
Reality Bites 12
Reservoir Dogs 8
Rock Around the Clock, 57
Romanticism 21–23, 48, 51, 63, 69, 97; and American culture 30–32, 42, 86–87

Sandler, Adam 79
Schwarzenegger, Arnold 76–77
sex, lies, and videotape 1, 8, 77
The Silence of the Lambs 94
Silent Bob 6, 52, 61, 86, 89–97
Singles 18, 22, 29
Smith, Kevin 1–3, 6, 23, 37, 60, 92–97; and Generation X 10; and masculinity 77, 86–87, 91; and Pop Culture 50–51

Soderbergh, Steven 1, 8–10
Soul Asylum 22, 95
soundtrack 4, 18–19, 21–22, 44–45, 89, 94–95
Spader, James 77
Spielberg, Steven 35
Spoonauer, Lisa *see* Bree, Caitlin
Stallone, Sylvester 76–77
Star Wars 14, 49, 51–52, 70, 93, 97
Star Wars: Episode II - Attack of the Clones 52
Star Wars: Episode V - The Empire Strikes Back 51, 70
Star Wars: Episode VI – Return of the Jedi 49, 51–52
subcultural capital 70–72, 94
Sundance Film Festival 1

Tarantino, Quentin 1, 8–9, 14–15
Teague, Lewis 68
television 10, 13–15, 50, 57, 59

Thoreau, Henry David 32, 42
Twain, Mark 31

Veblen, Thorstein 25, 29, 40–41, 68
Vermont 33, 45, 48
View Askewniverse 6, 86, 89, 92–96

Wake of Julie Dwyer 5, 52–54, 85, 88, 92
Washington Post 26–27, 73
Weinstein, Harvey and Bob 8
Whitaker, Forest 77
Willam (Snowball) 82
The Wizard of Oz 50
Woodstock Festival 12, 16, 24

youth subculture 6, 20, 32, 34, 39, 57, 63, 69–70
yuppies 58–59

Zustiak, Gary Blair 12–13

For Product Safety Concerns and Information please contact our EU representative GPSR@taylorandfrancis.com
Taylor & Francis Verlag GmbH, Kaufingerstraße 24, 80331 München, Germany

www.ingramcontent.com/pod-product-compliance
Lightning Source LLC
Chambersburg PA
CBHW070558170426
43201CB00012B/1873